SO-BOC-229

AMERICAN LABOR

FROM CONSPIRACY
TO
COLLECTIVE BARGAINING

ADVISORY EDITORS

Leon Stein   *Philip Taft*

THE NEGRO IN THE
SLAUGHTERING AND MEAT-PACKING
INDUSTRY IN CHICAGO

Alma Herbst

 ARNO & THE NEW YORK TIMES
New York   1971

Robert Manning Strozier **Library**

JAN 23 1976

Tallahassee, Florida

Reprint Edition 1971 by Arno Press Inc.

Reprinted from a copy in
The University of Illinois Library
LC# 73-156417
ISBN 0-405-02925-X

American Labor: From Conspiracy to Collective Bargaining—Series II
ISBN for complete set: 0-405-02910-1
See last pages of this volume for titles.

Manufactured in the United States of America

Hart, Schaffner & Marx Prize Essays

LII

THE NEGRO IN THE SLAUGHTERING AND MEAT-PACKING INDUSTRY IN CHICAGO

THE NEGRO
IN THE SLAUGHTERING
AND MEAT-PACKING
INDUSTRY IN
CHICAGO

BY

ALMA HERBST

BOSTON AND NEW YORK
HOUGHTON MIFFLIN COMPANY
1932

COPYRIGHT, 1932, BY HART, SCHAFFNER & MARX

ALL RIGHTS RESERVED INCLUDING THE RIGHT TO REPRODUCE
THIS BOOK OR PARTS THEREOF IN ANY FORM.

Printed in the United States of America by
J. J. LITTLE AND IVES COMPANY, NEW YORK

PREFACE

This series of books owes its existence to the generosity of Messrs. Hart, Schaffner & Marx, of Chicago, who have desired to encourage a wider interest in the study of economic and commercial subjects. For this purpose they have delegated to the undersigned committee the task of selecting or approving of topics, making announcements, and awarding prizes annually for those who wish to compete.

For the year 1930 there were offered:

In Class A, which included any American without restriction, a first prize of $1,000, and a second prize of $500.

In Class B, which included any who were at the time undergraduates of an American college, a first prize of $300, and a second prize of $200.

Any essay submitted in Class B, if deemed of sufficient merit, could receive a prize in Class A.

The present volume, submitted in Class A, was awarded Second Prize in 1930.

EDWIN F. GAY, *Chairman*
Harvard University

JOHN B. CLARK
Columbia University

WESLEY C. MITCHELL
Columbia University

AUTHOR'S PREFACE

The purpose of this study is to examine the status of Negro workmen in the slaughtering and meat-packing industry in Chicago. The inquiry centers about their entrance into the industry, the work they perform, their conditions of employment, their efficiency and reliability. The position and history of the industry is briefly sketched; the type of employment the industry affords, the amount of it which is available; the entrance and nationality succession of workers during labor controversies; the experience of the workers with trade-unionism. In the second half of the study an analysis appears of the data obtained from twenty-four slaughtering and meat-packing establishments, and finally a statistical analysis of the personnel of one meat-packing establishment over a four-year period.

The study could not have been undertaken or completed without the cooperation and aid of wage-earners, trade-union officials, employers, and members of the teaching staff of the University of Chicago. I am indebted to each of them. Grateful acknowledgment is given to Professor Harry A. Millis of the University of Chicago for his generous criticisms and helpful suggestions during every stage of the work. The project was sponsored and financed by the Local Community Research Committee of the University of Chicago.

ALMA HERBST

CONTENTS

PART III

A STUDY AND COMPARISON OF WHITE AND
NEGRO EMPLOYEES IN A TYPICAL MEAT-
PACKING ESTABLISHMENT

TABLES [1]

[1] See also Tables accompanying charts.

CHARTS AND ACCOMPANYING TABLES

INTRODUCTION

THE publicity which, during the early years of the century, was given to the sordid lives of the foreign-born living 'back of the yards,' whose existence was shaped and limited by the industrial processes of 'Packingtown,' was dramatic and emotional. It had no precedent and, as it has not been supplemented by similar accounts of other wage-earners, the impression persists that Slavic people, in particular Poles, have, in the main, constituted the packers' labor force. This is by no means the case. The Irish and Germans justly claim the distinction of having been the first packing house workers and of providing the yards with its most skilled and dexterous butchers. But the composition of the labor force did not remain intact in an expanding West where there was still 'room at the top' for the ambitious, assimilated and experienced workman, and the slaughtering and meat-packing industry was not the choice of those in a position to compete for jobs in an era of industrial expansion.

The invention of labor-saving machinery, coincident with the increased utilization of by-products, caused the mechanization and standardization of old tasks and the introduction of new ones. The industry, which had originally been two separate occupations of slaughtering and meat-packing, now became a related group of manufacturing operations bearing small resemblance to one another. In each the strategic positions requiring skilled workers were reduced and those to which the untrained could be added with facility increased. With the expansion of the industry between 1880 and 1890,[1] the chief task of the packing house employment officers was to obtain an ever increasing number of unskilled laborers, both absolutely and in proportion to the skilled. The qualifications for a job were a willingness to repeat a simple routine motion and the ability to comply with the demand for greater and greater celerity. People to whom other occupations were open did not take jobs of this char-

---

[1] United States Bureau of the Census, *Twelfth Census of the United States*, 1900, IX, Part III, pp. 388, 391.

acter. Hence the stockyards were manned chiefly by those who had no alternative—the most recent immigrants and Negroes.

In addition to this infiltration, however, a mass invasion by each succeeding nationality and racial group occurred during the labor controversies. The packers' easy immigrant and Negro labor market enabled them to secure a plentiful supply of manual laborers to supplant their striking employees. In 1886, 1894, 1904, and 1921, the hiring of strike-breakers was a prominent element in the defeat of the packing house workers. Furthermore, nationality and racial antagonisms and hatreds contributed to the division among workers, the disruption of labor organizations, and the establishment of the packers' non-union labor policy. Each new group of laborers, immigrant and Negro, increased its numerical strength in the industry at the same time that it contributed especially bitter elements to succeeding conflicts. Upon closer examination, however, the details of the strikes and subsequent events reveal fundamental dissimilarities in the operation and scope of racial differences as illustrated by the employment of the two groups. In the case of the foreign-born, the initial use of immigrants as strike-breakers presaged substantial gains in employment and advancement to semi-skilled, skilled, and supervisory positions. The racial antipathy excited by their first appearance could not be aroused so successfully in subsequent controversies, for a process of assimilation and adjustment soon began despite the fact that racial hatreds transplanted from overseas and the intense economic competition for jobs tended to perpetuate sharp racial cleavages in shop and community. Working side by side laborers became less suspicious of one another; they awakened to the need of common effort to improve their conditions of employment.

On the other hand, following their introduction into the plants, Negro strike-breakers made relatively minor gains in employment. Even when at last their race was able to supply the packers with enough workmen to aid materially in terminating the controversies and overthrowing the unions, permanent employment was not immediately within the reach of many. Gains in promotion and advancement were negligible. White men and women remained the preferred laborers. In successive controversies the presence of Negroes supplied growing racial hostility and antagonism which were accentuated by their increased employment following the heavy migrations from the South. As industrial opportunities were almost closed to Negroes, the packers found in them an available, ever larger group of manual laborers against whom the entire community was arrayed. An interesting exception occurred during the World War when their first industrial achievements were won; lucrative employment was so plentiful for white men that a welcome was extended even to Negroes within the stockyards. From 1918 to 1921, colored men were sought more whole-heartedly as trade-union members, and yet in the majority of cases they rejected the opportunity to affiliate with labor organizations. Following the armistice, in the keen competition for work, Negroes again found their employment and position in the yards dependent upon two circumstances divorced from industrial efficiency; namely, the restrictive immigration act, and the service they could still be counted upon to render in case further necessity arose to nip a labor organization of stockyard workers in the bud.

The part played by nationality differences is dramatized in the controversies of 1886, 1894, and 1904. The Negro first assumed the rôle of strike-breaker in 1894, having been coached by the workmen from southern Europe. He became outstandingly proficient on his own account as the defender and preserver of the packers' non-union labor policy in the strikes of 1904 and 1921, ever hoping thereby to realize the opportunities of permanent employment. Within this framework of conflict, competition, misunderstanding, and hostility, the status of the Negro was established and became crystallized.

The question of the efficiency of the Negro squarely presents itself. What kind of laborer is he? Are the slaughtering and meat-packing establishments handicapped in production by the necessity of employing him, despite his services of another nature? Is he to be used only in emergencies? That unskilled Negroes may be inefficient workmen is doubtless true. But the same thing was said of the

German, the Irishman, the Bohemian, the Pole, and the Lithuanian when he performed the work now done by the colored man and was the latest comer in the industry. Migrants who possess the heritage of 'cotton farmers,' illiterate and ignorant, are not at the outset in a position to be good factory workers. Industrial Negroes as a class suffer from the shortcomings of the individuals performing common labor during the period of adjustment. Although labor agents went South to bring Negro workers, whether employable or not, to the northern industries, and railways provided free transportation to anyone who was foot-loose and adventurous enough to leave, the skilled colored work-men of the South were also 'on the move,' impelled by the opportunities which were opening for them in many trades. But as long as one class of labor or one racial group con-tinues to furnish a preponderance of the applicants and supply the labor for the least attractive jobs and those most difficult to fill, so long will the ratings concerning them and their industrial incompetency react upon all members of the group. In proportion to the hosts of colored applicants ready to seize unskilled jobs, few Negroes occupy skilled positions. This situation operates to the disadvantage of the skilled; his position is precarious because it is affected by the rating, rate of wages, and inefficiency of the majority. In the case of the Negro, this is facilitated by the color of his skin which provides an easy means of identification. Furthermore, the difficulty the Negro experiences in finding other occupations, once he has proved himself and acquired the technique of an industrial system, subjects him to the limitations of the least effective workers of his race for a greater length of time than is the case with members of most nationality groups. Although Negro wage-earners may not be as efficient as white, it seems obvious that skilled Negroes on the killing floor must as surely keep up with the pace set by the sliding rail as the white butchers. And the almost total absence of work performed in individual units again necessitates a standard production by all members of groups, whether composed bi-racially or otherwise. Pace-setters among the working units allow for few individual incompetents.

However, racial considerations rather than statistical analysis, or an interpretation of economic factors, are not infrequently used in rating the productive capacity of Negroes. As a basis for the present examination of the status of the Negro workman in the slaughtering and meat-packing industry of Chicago, the industry which employs the largest number of wage-earners in the city, twenty-four establishments, embracing all branches of the industry, were selected. Both insignificant firms and those whose products bear internationally known trademarks were included. Within the twenty-four establishments, 27,869 wage-earners were employed, of whom 23,632, or 84.8 per cent, were men, and 4,237, or 15.2 per cent, were women. The racial composition was as follows: 16,727, or 70.8 per cent, of the men were white, and 6,905, or 29.2 per cent, were Negro; of the women, 3,111, or 73.4 per cent, were white, and 1,126, or 26.6 per cent, were Negro.

The Chicago slaughtering and meat-packing firms maintain an open door to the visitor who seeks information concerning their wage-earners. The vastness of the industry and the thousands upon thousands of workers permit few secrets in respect of employment conditions; employers and workers aid in providing information. In almost every case more than one representative of each establishment and several hundred wage-earners were interviewed. The officials to whom the investigator was referred included presidents, personnel and employment secretaries, general superintendents, and foremen; they varied in their interest, their desire to coöperate, and in their ability to give authentic information, but replied without much hesitation to questions concerning the employment conditions of white and Negro wage-earners. In no instance was an attempt made to defend or justify existing practices or policies. Although rarely approached with questions concerning Negro laborers, the officials readily made statements regarding them, not infrequently going into great detail. The general agreement in the material thus secured fell into a definite pattern which served as the justification for a statistical analysis of the records of certain establishments.

Since 1921 the proportion of Negro workers in the packing houses has generally fluctuated around 30 per cent of the total plant help. During the World War, of the total number of employees the percentage of Negroes rose in a few cases to as high as 70 or 80. The chief reason for employing colored workers cited by every establishment was the fear of trade-unionism and of labor difficulties. In case of future strikes or attempts to unionize the butchers, the packers were counting upon the Negro 'to see them through' as he did in 1904 and in 1921. With this in view, colored workers have been distributed in the key departments and occupations and some have thus attained positions of highest skill in the yards. Nevertheless the majority still fall well within the category of unskilled laborers. In most of the plants racial attitudes rather than actual performance were frequently felt to determine the status of the Negro in the industry and to define his place; generalizations, dogmas, and myths concerning the Negro's industrial efficiency and his treatment were combined with statements of preference for white workers.

The period of mass invasion of the slaughtering and meat-packing industry by Negroes has come to an end. Since the introduction of Mexicans into the yards to fill the gaps in the ranks of the unskilled, they can no longer be looked upon as the last-comers to the establishments. The period of speculation concerning their ability to make good and to prove themselves as acceptable wage-earners has also closed. Their performance is sufficient to put an end to conjecture; they have gained experience, and with it, proficiency in a trade. But despite the achievement, their position and status remain unassured and precarious; they are again in a predicament, one in which new problems, fears, and barriers loom ominously. They are making no gains in the industry. In fact, economic forces, affecting the employment of all workers, have brought a relatively greater diminution in the number of Negro workmen in the slaughtering and meat-packing establishments. As production is curtailed and unemployment sweeps the city, they are fighting for their jobs—for the unskilled stockyard work—which in Chicago has become traditionally 'Negro.' Brought by necessity, an increasing number of white men are re-

placing Negroes, who are, in turn, shifting to more diversi-
fied occupations in the community than at any previous time.

But even at the moment of temporary reversal, colored
workmen are aware of their gains, and of the approaching
competition for jobs which will soon occur between individuals of the two racial groups.   The transition of the
Negro from agricultural and domestic service to industrial
was brought about by emergencies in the industrial life of
the nation; the second phase in their industrial experience
will transcend the first in social and economic consequence.
Although the Negroes in the one establishment studied in
detail verified the experience of those in other slaughtering
and meat-packing firms in the yards, that they feel themselves more nearly on a competitive equality with white
workers than in any other industry in the city, yet antagonisms and fears appear as men prepare to enter economic
competition in an industry of a city rife with racial prejudices which have not been overcome by either workers or
employers.

THE NEGRO IN THE SLAUGHTER-ING AND MEAT-PACKING INDUSTRY IN CHICAGO

PART I

THE SETTING

CHAPTER I

FACTORS AFFECTING EMPLOYMENT IN THE INDUSTRY

In Chicago, concentrated within one square mile, lies the largest livestock market in the world.[1] It is a place of paradox: of beauty and color, filth and degradation; of the essence of scientific and engineering attainment, yet raw and primitive.· In 1928, one hundred and one slaughtering and meat-packing establishments were located within the Union Stock Yards and in the adjoining neighborhood, ranging in size from three small plants in which less than twenty workmen were employed to one of over ten thousand. In these one hundred and one houses, 33,281 persons had employment, of whom 28,323, or 85.1 per cent, were men, and 4,958, or 14.9 per cent, were women.

Three elements inherent in the slaughtering and meat-packing industry affect the nature of employment within it and must be examined in a study endeavoring to ascertain the status of the Negro among its employees: first, the inevitable conditions and distasteful circumstances attending the work; second, the high degree to which economy in the slaughtering of cattle has been carried by means of standardization and subdivision of tasks; and third, seasonality. The combination of these factors leads to a continuous procession of cheap, unskilled wage-earners through the establishments, makes for irregularity of employment, and an increase in the percentage of common laborers in the industry. The simplicity of operations has made possible the utilization of hordes of newcomers and surplus marginal workers, as well as of unemployed and unemployables, who have turned to the stockyards as a last resort.

[1] Figures showing the growth of the industry and its concentration in Chicago appear in Tables XXVII, XXVIII, XXIX, XXX, XXXI, XXXII in Appendix A.

I

The three main reasons for the continued unpleasantness of the work are to be found in, first, the nature of slaughtering and meat-packing operations; second, the antiquated condition of some of the buildings and premises; and third, the availability of an abundant and cheap supply of unskilled labor.

Noisy, bleating, bellowing, or mute, intimidated cattle, hogs, and sheep, in a seemingly interminable procession are driven from the stockyards to the packing houses; suspended from overhead, on sliding rails, they pass before silent, dexterous workers in the killing and dressing departments; shaven or skinned, cleaned and inspected, they enter the great coolers. Cattle complete the journey in thirty-two minutes; the smaller animals are dispatched with greater celerity. The daily killing capacity in one of the largest abattoirs is 3,600 cattle, 10,800 hogs, 10,000 sheep, and 8,450 calves. Within forty-eight hours the carcasses are ready to be brought from the coolers; operations are not slackened until an animal has been completely utilized. The application of scientific chemical, and industrial research, the manufacture of by-products, the adoption of the most efficient labor-saving devices, the elimination of waste have made this possible.

But these achievements in organization and the consequent adjustments in conditions of employment cannot alter the nature of the raw materials or of the numerous tasks in which human labor is utilized, nor eliminate the nauseating smells, the cries of stricken animals, the streams of warm blood, and tons of raw meat; the trade is still butchering and packing.

In the second place, the disagreeableness of the occupation is the result of physical conditions within the packing houses which have accumulated over an extended period.[1] Since the founding of the houses in the Union Stock Yards, each new technical achievement in slaughtering, packing, and the

---

[1] The earliest accounts of the industry contain references to the filth and stench both within the enclosures and the neighboring community. Previous to

utilization of by-products has been adopted. But the premises within which operations have been conducted have received a minimum of renovation and improvement. Today the relative dominance of Chicago over other packing centers [1] operates to diminish economic incentive to improve either the nature of the work or the conditions under which it is performed. Conditions are not uniform and to some extent buildings and equipment have been repaired, renovated, or entirely replaced and the physical surroundings of some employees materially improved by a strict segregation of the more obnoxious portions of the work. But many tasks demand the constant use of running water and of steam, a wide range in temperature, an excessive degree of dampness and humidity. Too much of the old still remains, making glaring contrasts with the new: the white-tiled, scientific pharmaceutical laboratory and the dreary, stinking hole in which entrails are cleaned; the modern, light killing room and the cold, dark cutting and trimming departments; the clean, tiled, and well-ventilated rooms in which peanuts are shelled and an original soup and canning kitchen, heavy with steam, whose small sooty windows the sun tries in vain to penetrate; the long, slippery, dark hallways and staircases leading from the most modern departments to dark, ill-

---

the construction of the old 'Bull's Head Market' in 1848, at Ashland Avenue and Madison Street, the cattle and hogs were dumped on the sand hills and sold at so much per head. In 1856, the Sherman Yards, located on the Myrick property on the lake shore at Thirty-First Street and on the Illinois Central and Michigan Central Railroads, were opened. The Michigan Southern Railroad had opened a yard at State and Twenty-Second Streets in 1854; the Fort Wayne, at Steward and Mitchell Streets, in 1859; the Cottage Grove Yards in 1862; the Burlington Yards in 1865. The Civil War, bringing increased business to the packing industry, accentuated the need for adequate, well-built, and centralized cattle-pens in the city of Chicago. On Christmas Day, 1865, the Union Stock Yards of Chicago were opened. Three hundred and twenty acres of marsh land in the Town of Lake were purchased from John Wentworth for $100,000. The location was deemed especially favorable because of the great distance from the city and the opportunity the river provided for direct means of sewage disposal. 'Bubbly Creek,' the hair fields and dumps soon formed the boundaries of Lake Michigan's hinterland known as 'Packingtown.' Alfred T. Andreas, *History of Chicago* (Chicago: The A. T. Andreas Co., 1884-86), I, pp. 122, 554, 560-61, 563-64; II, pp. 553-54; III, p. 334; Rudolph A. Clemen, *The American Livestock and Meat Industry* (New York: The Ronald Press Co., 1923), pp. 102-03; *The Autobiography of Gordon S. Hubbard* (Chicago: The Lakeside Press, 1911), pp. 177-78.

[1] A shift in the corn-growing states and grazing centers, new developments in refrigeration, the emergence of coöperative societies, and direct buying and selling methods have resulted in a corresponding shift in the development of packing centers.

ventilated rooms, not infrequently lacking a coat of white-wash or fresh paint.

Nor has a dearth of workers forced the packers to make employment as attractive as possible. Success in obtaining cheap, common laborers facilitated further specialization, mechanization, speed, a disregard for conditions of employment. The situation was cumulative in its effects. Two groups of unskilled laborers gratefully accept work in the yards, those who are hard-pressed temporarily, and those who look upon it as the best opportunity for entering the industrial field. Women workers, fearing loss of status, frequently conceal their occupations of trimming, sausage-stuffing, chitterling-washing; skilled workmen do not boast of their technique. Although successive immigrant groups and Negroes are always on hand to perform the disagreeable work, every labor manager knows that the very circumstance which affords the packers an easy labor market is responsible for the high labor turnover.

II

Division of labor, which has a long history in the slaughtering and meat-packing industry,[1] kept pace with the utilization of by-products,[2] the concentration, and the localization of the industry; 'robots' became the preferred workmen. And within the department which was and is the core of the industry—the killing and dressing of livestock—division of labor shows its greatest development and most distinctive features. The killing and dressing of cattle is a part of a

---

[1] Clemen, op. cit., p. 122; Harriet Martineau, Retrospect of Western Travel (London: Saunders and Otley, 1838), II, p. 45.

[2] The outstanding features fundamental to the development of Chicago's packing industry appeared shortly after the benefits of the railroad began to be felt. These consisted of the combination of slaughtering and packing, the livestock market, the commission firms, the discovery of the refrigeration process and its application to the car. The sudden and unprecedented use of by-products came after the adoption of refrigeration. From 1880 to 1890, the growth in the value of the products was 85 per cent and of the cost of materials 79.6 per cent. The packers increased the value of their products more rapidly than the livestock dealers could adjust their prices. (United States Bureau of the Census, Twelfth Census of the United States, 1900, IX, Part III, pp. 387-88.) In 1886 the first chemist was installed. Clemen, op. cit., chap. XVI; and By-Products in the Packing Industry (Chicago: The University of Chicago Press, 1927).

disassembling handicraft, as contrasted with the assembling processes in most manufacturing pursuits. Despite the fact that with few exceptions all tasks in this department must be performed by hand, here has been realized the most outstanding triumph for the principles of standardization, routine, and specialization. The tools are the knife, saw, cleaver, and ax, most of which are owned by the workers. In a few exceptional instances, electricity has been applied to increase the speed and efficiency of an operation.

For those whose natural aptitudes lay in the direction of dexterity with the knife, division of labor facilitated the development of greater skill. Their technique became localized and concentrated. The most efficient cattle butchers in the world lived in the community. A prerogative of family groups, though changing with successive immigrant waves, the tradition was passed on from father to son. An aristocracy was created; each cattle butcher drove his own horse and buggy, and donned a high hat when occasion demanded. His life was bounded by his occupation and the community which lived back of the yards.

The moving conveyor brought about specialization in the minute processes of the craft. Companies coöperated in exchanging data from their experiments. When a job permitted no further simplification, production could be augmented by accelerating the speed of the moving conveyor. Speed could be increased to the point at which there was danger of slashing hides. The technique of the cattle butcher was dissipated, diminished, or made into a craft in which a group participated. Workers now kept pace with the speed set by the sliding rail. The operations requiring the most skill were refined in such a way that the most dexterous worker did only the most difficult and exacting portion; he performed only part of the work he had formerly handled, and became highly specialized.[1] Several inferior workers were put upon the less difficult tasks.

This change in the trade of the cattle butcher was not

[1] John R. Commons, 'Labor Conditions in Meat Packing and the Recent Strike,' *The Quarterly Journal of Economics*, XIX (1904-05), pp. 3-4. A gang of 230 men killing 105 cattle an hour were paid as follows: 11 men were paid 50 cents an hour; 3, 45 cents; 86, 20 cents and over; 144 were paid under 20 cents.

unique among packing house occupations. The chief effects of the division of labor were, first, that it now became economically desirable for the packers to employ large quantities of unskilled and immigrant labor, among whom were numbers of women and children.[1] In the second place, the skill and wages of a few were increased. For a time the skilled workers were flattered and misled by their increased importance. Put on steady weekly time, they received higher wages and better positions. They did not foresee that this monopoly of key positions and of the best conditions of employment, in which they acted as 'pace-setters' and 'speeders-up,' was to act as a boomerang, nor could they have changed the course of events had they been able to realize this. Speeding-up, the third consequence, ensued.[2] The dependence of the employers on a few specialized operators in each department rendered them relatively independent of the hordes of common laborers. But the increase in the number of the latter augmented their importance.

From 1900 to 1905, speeding-up and division of labor reached their highest development.[3] In 1905, a report on the Beef Industry from the Commissioner of Corporations

[1] In 1850, for the United States as a whole, the industry employed 9 women; in 1860, 19 women; in 1870, 202 women and 258 children. In 1880, no women were employed in the industry and the number of children increased 358.9 per cent, to 1,184. Meat canning was started in 1875; women gained a hold on this work from 1880 to 1890. In the latter year 990 women and 700 children were employed. (*Twelfth Census of the United States*, 1900, IX, Part III, p. 387.) An account of the work of women in the yards in 1888 is contained in *The Chicago Tribune*, 'Nora's Stockyards Fun,' November 25, 1888. For a discussion of the entrance of women into the stockyards and the conditions of their employment, see Edith Abbott and S. P. Breckinridge, 'Women in Industry: The Chicago Stockyards,' *Journal of Political Economy*, 1911, XIX, pp. 632-54; Dennis Lane, *United States Commission on Industrial Relations*, Final Report and Testimony, 1916, IV, p. 3518; Michael Donnelly, *Official Journal*, Amalgamated Meat Cutters and Butcher Workmen of North America, May, 1906, p. 30. The employment of boys is described in the following references: *Second Annual Report of the Factory Inspectors of Illinois*, 1894, pp. 20, 21; *Third Annual Report of the Factory Inspectors of Illinois*, 1895, pp. 10-11.

[2] Commons, *op. cit.*, pp. 6-7.

[3] *Ibid.*, pp. 7, 15. In 1884, five splitters on a cattle-killing gang would get out 800 cattle in 10 hours, or 16 per hour per splitter. Wages were 45 cents an hour. In 1894, 4 splitters got out 1,200 cattle in 10 hours, or 30 per hour per splitter, an increase of almost 100 per cent. The wages for all except the steady-time men were reduced to 40 cents per hour. The pace-setters on a gang of sheep butchers were the pelters and the setters. One pelter and one setter in a gang were formerly steady-time men. The speed of the pelter had been pushed to 60 and even 75 sheep per hour. The speed was

showed that at one of the great abattoirs 157 men were working on a beef-killing gang handling the cattle killed by two knockers and one sticker. The number does not include the men and women making the by-products, or those operating the power or refrigerating machinery. These 157 men performed no fewer than 78 distinct operations and could take care of more than a thousand cattle in a ten-hour day.[1]

III

In spite of extended use of refrigeration,[2] the packer has never been able to eliminate the effects of the weather upon his products, over which he has control only while they are within his own establishment.[3] He has done much to regulate and improve the amount, kind, and time of shipment of livestock into the Union Stock Yards. No longer are the heavy shipments confined to the first days of the week, and

limited by the union prior to the strike of 1904 to 46 per hour; and the companies placed all the steady-time men on the hourly basis.

[1] See Appendix C.

[2] Ice packing was begun very cautiously in 1857. The next improvement came in the use of refrigerating machines. In 1874, the first large 'chill room' in the world was built at Armour's Chicago plant. From 1870 to 1880, large chill rooms and refrigerator machinery were installed in the Chicago packing plants, and refrigerator cars were used extensively. In March, 1879, by means of refrigerator cars and vessels, meat was shipped to England. Before 1870, summer slaughtering and packing were almost negligible in the United States. Contrasting the packing year 1872-73 with 1879-80, the summer packing amounted to 8.5 per cent of the packing for the entire year during the earlier period, but grew to 37.7 per cent in the latter; 505,500 hogs were slaughtered during the summer season in 1872-73, and 4,051,248 in 1879-80. For these same packing years winter packing increased 28.5 per cent; and summer packing, 701.6 per cent. From 1870 to 1880 the per cent of increase in the cost of materials, the value of products, the average number of wage-earners, and the total wages was larger than for any other decade of the century. *Twelfth Census of the United States*, 1900, IX, Part III, pp. 387-88, 421.

[3] When the 'Consent Decree' was signed February 27, 1920, the possibility of developing side lines to meet the problem of the industry was limited. (United States *v.* Swift and Company, *et al.*, 37623 Equity, Washington, Government Printing Office, 1920. As quoted in Clemen, *op. cit.*, pp. 783-84.) The Palmer-Packer Agreement and the 'Consent Decree' compelled the packers to dispose of their interests in public stockyards, stockyard terminals and railroads, market papers, cold storage warehouses, to disassociate themselves from all 'unrelated lines,' including wholesale groceries, fresh, canned, and salt fish, canned fruit and vegetables, and certain other products, to abandon the use of their distributive systems for other than their own meat and dairy products. The packers were allowed to continue their production and sale of cottonseed oil, oleo, butter, cheese, eggs, and poultry. This decree was the forerunner of the Packers and Stockyards Act of 1921, which placed the regulation of the industry within the jurisdiction of the Secretary of Agriculture.

to a few months. The rancher or farmer has learned that it
is to his advantage to spread his sales over the year. But
the marketing habits of livestock dealers are well established, and in turn dependent upon natural conditions over
which their control is limited. Once the product has been
received by the packing establishment, the benefits of refrigeration which center in cold storage can be realized. The
packer has to a lesser degree controlled seasonality by another method—that of holding back certain less perishable
or non-perishable portions of the carcass in order to spread
the work over periods when the run of cattle, hogs, and sheep
slackens. In the demand and consumption of meat and
produce also he has learned to meet seasonal, in addition to
sectional and geographic variations. The consumer has
been beseeched through enticing advertisements to use picnic
hams, summer sausage, chops, and light roasts in warm
weather, and the heavier cuts of meat in winter. A distinct summer product has been developed, put upon the
market, and a demand created for it.

Nevertheless, seasonality has come to be thought of as an
inherent and imperious inconvenience which the industry
must anticipate—a symbol, a sufficient explanation to offer
in placing responsibility for grievances in regard to almost
any unsatisfactory condition of employment. Throughout
'Packingtown' the busiest season is about the last week in
November, during December, or early January. Lay-offs
begin then and the depression lasts through the summer
months. Ordinarily in July or August the run of livestock
picks up. Workers who have been transferred to other
departments are then restored to their original positions and
wage-earners are taken on until the peak of employment is
again reached. Although the magnitude of variation between these periods of high and low employment has been
lessened, they have not been eliminated and recur annually.

Until recently the packer has accepted lack of security,
under-employment, and absence of 'hope on the job' as the
inevitable tolls exacted of the hourly workers by the nature
of the industry.[1] Today his answer to employees who
charge irregularity of employment is the guarantee of pay

[1] Part III, Chapter VII, p. 127 ff.

for forty hours in any one week to those who are kept on the payroll. But this is realized only by the few on the trained force who are kept busy by interdepartmental transfer during the slack season. The cattle butchers seldom experience either a lay-off or a temporary allocation to another department or occupation, but members of the killing gang and the semi-skilled workers are not so fortunate. The choice of a lay-off or a division of time between their own occupation and that of another, invariably requiring a lesser degree of craft and technique, is their lot. Although many unskilled workers are required the year round, common laborers have come to think of the employment offered by the packers in terms of the lay-off they are certain to meet with at least once a year.

Negro men and white and Negro women suffer most heavily. In the plant studied, the minimum number of white men employed at any one time between 1922 and 1926 was about two-thirds of the maximum whereas only one-third as many Negro women were on the payroll during the slack season as during the busy.

CHAPTER II

THE COMING OF THE NEGRO

From 1820 to 1890 the major proportion of immigrants came from the north and west European countries.[1] Eighteen eighty-two, the year of unprecedented immigration, marked the beginning of an important shift in the nationality distribution. The fact is doubly significant because the decade from 1880 to 1890 outsripped all others of the century in the number of new arrivals in the United States. The people from southern, central, and eastern Europe, especially those from Italy, Russia, Finland, and Austria-Hungary, now became the most important factors in the new movement of nationalities.[2]

In the eighties industries expanded enormously as machine production and the factory system were introduced. Semi-skilled and unskilled foreign laborers could be utilized, and not infrequently found that employers preferred them to Americans, including second-generation immigrants, who were now affiliating with labor organizations. The representatives of the new immigration brought lower standards of living. The movement of population was from country to city; new arrivals concentrated in industrial areas. An end had come to the great westward movement into the unoccupied public domain; the 'frontier of settlement' was said to have disappeared. Industrial opportunities super-

[1] United States Immigration Commission, *Reports of the Immigration Commission*, III, p. 12.
[2] Germans ranked first in the number of immigrants arriving in the United States from 1854 to 1894 inclusive, excluding the years 1863 and 1864. In 1900, Germany dropped to sixth place and yielded her position to Austria-Hungary; Italy stepped into second place; Russia, third. (*Reports of the Immigration Commission*, III, pp. 25-40.) A comparison of the two decades from 1881 to 1890, and from 1891 to 1900, shows in the latter period the following increase in immigration: from Italy, 112.1 per cent; from the Russian Empire and Finland, 119.6 per cent; and from Austria-Hungary, 67.6 per cent. The number decreased from 1891 to 1900: from England, 66.4 per cent; from the German Empire, 65.2 per cent; from Ireland, 40.7 per cent; from Sweden, 42.2 per cent. *United States Census Report, Statistics of Women at Work*, 1900, p. 51.

seded agricultural openings as the incentive of the immigrant.

The Chicago slaughtering and meat-packing industry experienced the economic and social changes of the period.
Parallel with the immigrant waves to the United States from
northern, western, southern, and southeastern Europe runs
the occupational succession of immigrants into the industry.
After 1875, which marked the extension in the use of by-
products and a realization of the economies and benefits of
refrigeration, more and more tasks of a monotonous, routine, and irksome nature were open. Seasonal jobs, filthy
and disagreeable, unskilled and heavy, repetitious within
narrow limits, could and would be performed by the latest
arrival who sought the work which the Old World had
failed to provide. And the job, as seen by others, became
undesirable, largely because the immigrant accepted it.

By the close of the nineteenth century, a revolution had
taken place in the technique of slaughtering and packing
livestock. The state and the city maintained their respective
positions of preëminence; refrigeration cars delivered the
packers' products to remote markets. Branch houses were
established throughout the country. As the growing middle-
western city became the center of the industry's operations,[1]
the packers' labor demands rose from 2,129 'hands' in 1869
to 25,478 wage-earners (average) [2] in 1899. At first, as successive immigrants took the most disagreeable jobs, the least
skilled laborer about the yards was not averse to seeing
another man willing to do his work. His position seemed
for a time bettered thereby, for he progressed to semi-skilled
work. Whatever rivalry and opposition did arise were found
only where sheer competition for jobs occurred, and it was

[1] The supremacy of Chicago in the slaughtering and meat-packing industry,
including all its branches, dates from 1861-62, when it took the lead from
Cincinnati. (*Twelfth Census of the United States*, IX, Part III, p. 414.) In
1925, the claim of packing as the city's outstanding industry is supported by
evidence which rates it first among the industries in the community on the
basis of the number of wage-earners employed, the cost of material utilized,
and the value of products; and second, on the amount of its payroll. Only
in the number of its establishments, which is an index of its concentration,
does it rank considerably below other industries and competes with two others
for the seventeenth place. *Census of Manufactures: 1925, Statistics for Industries, States and Cities*, pp. 111-14.

[2] See Table XXVIII, p. 152 and footnote * to Table XXVII, p. 151.

as a more or less natural defense reaction that bitterness, hostility, and race prejudice ensued.

Between 1880 and 1890, the first adverse results of the heavy immigration were felt by the workers in the packing industries. In 1886, the majority were still American-born, Germans, Irish, English, and Scandinavians. Among the butchers, Germans and Irish led, followed closely by workers from the British Empire and the native-born.[1] Laborers who had suffered from the depression of 1884-85 resented the intrusion of the new arrivals who now underbid them for jobs. Foreigners became objects of suspicion; a clash, the origin of which was partly economic, partly social, became imminent.

And so at the time when Chicago was flooded with newly arrived immigrants from southern Europe seeking employment, and the meat-packing industry was organized to employ them in all but a few important positions, the workers joined in the movement for the eight-hour day.[2] On May 3, headed by John T. Joyce and the leading cattle butchers, with little or no formal organization, they gained their demands—the former ten hours' pay for eight hours of work.[3] They came off somewhat better than most partici-

[1] *Reports of the Immigration Commission,* 'Immigrants in Industries,' XIII (1911), pp. 199-206. In 1886 a study of the labor organizations of Illinois was made, revealing the fact that of the 1,200 butchers in trade organizations, 700 were Germans, 300 were Irish, 100 were English, 50 were Scandinavian, and 50 American-born. In a summary of the Illinois industries, the Germans surpassed all others in membership in trade unions; the American-born, who were second, were nearly equaled by the Irish. The Knights of Labor had a membership relatively larger among the American-born. The Germans and the Irish constituted one-third of the membership of the Knights of Labor, the former being more numerous. The entire membership of the various labor organizations, subdivided as to nationalities, was as follows: Americans, 32 per cent; Germans, 27 per cent; Irish, 17 per cent; Scandinavians, 9 per cent; English, Scotch, and Welsh, 9 per cent; and Poles, Bohemians, and Italians, 6 per cent. *Report of the Bureau of Labor Statistics of Illinois,* 1886, pp. 224-30.

[2] For an account of the labor controversies in the yards, see Edna Louise Clark, *History of the Controversy Between Labor and Capital in the Slaughtering and Meat-Packing Industries in Chicago.* (Unpublished Master's Thesis, University of Chicago, 1922.)

[3] The packing house workers were identified with the Knights of Labor. The strike was only one in the more general movement to gain the eight-hour day, which was the outstanding plank in the program of the Federation of Organized Trades and Labor Unions of the United States and Canada and falteringly endorsed by the Knights of Labor. *Report of the Fourth Annual Session,* Federation of Organized Trades and Labor Unions of the United States and Canada, held at Chicago, Illinois, October 7, 8, 9, 10, 1884, pp. 19-20, 24-25; *Record of the Proceedings of the Ninth Regular Ses-*

pants in the strikes for the eight-hour day,[1] for they had settled with the packers before the Haymarket Riots.[2] All activities of labor groups were now identified with the Socialists, who were held responsible for the violence. Denunciations were heaped upon them and upon non-English-speaking people.[3] An anti-foreign hysteria seized the people of Chicago.

Within five months the employers announced that, on October 11, 1886, the ten-hour day would be resumed.[4] The 'Poles,' an appellation fastened on all newcomers from southern and southeastern Europe, were used as strike-breakers during the lockout which terminated on November 13 in the complete disruption of the labor organization.[5] This affront, the importation of immigrant scabs, combined with the employment of Pinkerton men armed with revolvers and Winchester rifles, increased the growing enmity between the packers and their workers.[6]

sion, General Assembly of the Knights of Labor, held at Hamilton, Ontario, October 5-13, 1885, Document 106, p. 125; Document 127, p. 128; p. 135; Terence V. Powderly, *Thirty Years of Labor* (Columbus, Ohio: Excelsior Printing House, 1890), pp. 483, 493.

[1] Bradstreet's reported that in 22 cities shorter hours were gained by 111,000 workers; the largest number in a single industry to receive the eight-hour day was 35,000 in Chicago's slaughtering and meat-packing industry. *The Chicago Tribune,* May 8, 1886, p. 2.

[2] Accounts of the movement to gain an eight-hour day, the strike, and the Haymarket Riots are contained in *The Chicago Tribune,* May 1, 1886, pp. 1, 2, 4; May 2, 1886, pp. 4, 9, 11, 17; May 3, 1886, pp. 1, 2, 4; May 4, 1886, pp. 1, 2, 3; May 5, 1886, pp. 1, 2, 3, 4; May 6, 1886, pp. 1, 2, 3, 4, 5; *The Chicago Daily News (The Morning News),* May 1, 1886, pp. 1, 2, 4; May 3, 1886, p. 1; May 4, 1886, p. 1; May 5, 1886, pp. 1, 5; May 6, 1886, pp. 1, 2; May 7, 1886, p. 1; May 8, 1886, p. 1.

[3] Eight men stood trial for the throwing of the bomb at the Haymarket Riots, five of whom were German immigrants, a sixth, an American of German parentage; three of the four who were hanged were Germans.

[4] *The Chicago Daily News (The Morning News),* October 8, 1886, p. 4. The packers realized that public sentiment was with them; that the number of organized workers was very small indeed, and that these were not whole-heartedly supported by their national organization. (*Report of the Bureau of Labor Statistics of Illinois,* 1886, pp. 173, 179, 235, 238.) In the five months' interim, the packers had formed a strong combination headed by Mr. J. Ogden Armour.

[5] The loss of the stockyard strike had a marked effect in hastening the decline of the power of the Knights of Labor throughout the United States. General Workman T. V. Powderly misused the authority of a highly centralized organization. It was claimed, moreover, that he followed the advice of Father Flannigan, priest of the Catholic Church at Fifty-Fifth Street and Wentworth Avenue, rather than that of the officers of the Knights of Labor.

[6] *The Chicago Tribune,* October 9, 1886, p. 8; October 12, 1886, p. 5; October 14, 1886, p. 8; October 17, 1886, p. 14; November 9, 1886, p. 1; *The Chicago Daily News (The Morning News),* October 11, 1886, p. 4; October 16, 1886, p. 3; October 18, 1886, p. 1; *The Chicago Herald,* October

Entering the district in 1884,[1] few Poles were employed about the yards before 1886.[2] Unskilled laborers, they were not sought as members of the Knights of Labor. And to see these foreigners who had acted as strike-breakers usurp their places was extremely distasteful to the Irish, Americans, Germans, and Scotch. The Poles were first employed in the making of fertilizer and in the hide cellars, but soon shared in all unskilled work. By 1894 they had fairly monopolized the jobs lowest in the scale.[3] Bohemians, who preceded the Poles into the yards by two years, easily outstripped them and advanced to the semi-skilled and skilled work. The neighborhood changed.[4] Sections immediately adjoining the yards, occupied by English-speaking people and Germans, were slowly invaded. Poles were joined by Slovaks, Ruthenians, Magyars, Croatians, Slovenians, Servians, and Syrians.[5] Stockyard laborers settled in close proximity to their work; congested, segregated immigrant communities came into existence. The Irish and Germans moved farther south.

II

In 1881, two men among all the employees in 'little Nels', the cattle king's, packing company' of Chicago, were conspicuous for their color—Freddie Lewis, the butcher,

16, 1886, p. 1; *The Sunday Herald,* October 17, 1886, p. 1; *The Chicago Evening Telegram,* October 18, 1886, p. 1; October 19, 1886, p. 1.

[1] *Reports of the Immigration Commission,* XIII, p. 200.

[2] Contradiction of this is found in Carroll D. Wright, 'Influence of Trade-Unionism on Immigrants,' *Bulletin of the Bureau of Labor,* X (1905), p. 2: 'The Poles began to come into the Yards in 1886, after the settlement of the strike, but not as strike-breakers. This appears to have been a voluntary immigration, increasing in volume until by 1890 the most of the unskilled occupations were filled by Poles, who by 1894 had practical control of the common labor.'

[3] In 1890, of 3,093 butchers in the Chicago meat-packing and slaughtering industry, 1,609 were German; 329 were Irish; 321 were British; 161 were Scandinavian. *Eleventh Census of the United States,* 1890, I², pp. 650-51.

[4] Workers were dismissed if suspected of membership in a labor organization. Many of the skilled workers left because of the following agreement which they were forced to sign on returning: 'The packer agrees to employ the old hand in the capacity of ———, wages to be ———, and the service to continue only so long as satisfactory to the packer. The employee agrees to give at least two weeks' notice of his intention to leave, and, as a guarantee of his intention to carry out the agreement, agrees to deposit the sum of ——— with the packer and forfeit the said sum should he violate any of the conditions of the agreement. Said sums to be retained out of the first weeks' wages.' *The Chicago Tribune,* November 12, 1886, p. 2.

[5] *Reports of the Immigration Commission,* XIII, pp. 199-200.

and his brother, the beef-boner.[1] Until the nineties, no mention of the Negro as a group is made in the literature dealing with the laborers in the yards,[2] nor were many Negroes found in the northern labor market. The few who entered the larger packing houses in the early nineties introduced no elements of conflict or competition. Negro butchers were an oddity; even unskilled Negro laborers were few. To stand beside a black man was an unfamiliar experience which at first created an element of curiosity and interest rather than of conflict. Nevertheless, in 1894 in the competition for jobs, including that of strike-breaking, this friendly contact changed to one of dislike and hatred. The Pullman strike of that year brought a realization to the packers and workmen that Negroes were potential stockyard laborers. Just as the introduction of workmen from southern and southeastern Europe into the yards to supplant strikers gave an added element of animosity to the controversy of 1886, so also did the interpenetration of Negro scabs (joined to immigrant laborers) add this racial hatred and antagonism to later strikes.

Although not a struggle primarily between the packers and their employees, the sympathetic strike of 1894 was in many respects the most important in the annals of the yards. Contrary to the situation presented by the lockout of 1886, when, despite the destruction of the labor organization, the workers were not without success in registering protest against conditions of employment, in 1894 they were misled and duped into joining a losing fight.[3] In the Pullman struggle which they joined the incentives which inspired them were not those of Mr. Debs. Such influences were too remote; the stockyard workers fought against United States troops and against one another. This struggle of worker against worker was repeated in every subsequent controversy. The Poles, who were again the first strike-

---

[1] Previous to this time Negro laborers were employed in larger numbers in Kansas City by Armour and Company and Swift and Company.

[2] *Bulletin of the Bureau of Labor,* X (1905), p. 2. In 1890, one Negro was a member of Armour's killing gang.

[3] The 'Debs Strike,' the American Railway Union's struggle with the Pullman Company, was called on May 11. The newly formed butchers' union joined a sympathetic strike called on July 9. The butchers were a recent addition to the Knights of Labor and claimed a membership of 1,600.

breakers coming to the assistance of the employers, competed with Austrians, Russians, Croatians, Servians, and Magyars. Within four days of the calling of the strike, however, mention was made of Negroes. Their first offer of help was rejected,[1] but in a few more days they were being brought into the yards.[2]

The strike was characterized by lawlessness and retaliation. The yards swarmed with workers of every nationality seeking employment. From 2,000 to 8,000 disappointed laborers were kept moving at the point of fixed bayonets through the streets of 'Packingtown.'[3] Destitute women with canvas sacks followed the men to the yards, picking up small pieces of meat that chanced to fall to the ground at the loading platforms.[4] The general cry was for vengeance against non-union men and especially Negroes. As a protective measure strike-breakers were housed in the meat-packing establishments.[5] Not only were the Negroes threatened and their effigies burned, but attacks upon them were numerous.

Incendiaries fired the wholesale meat warehouse of Nelson Morris & Co. . . . late last night. . . . There were four companies of infantry and two of cavalry under arms in the yards. How the sentinels managed to let an incendiary through the lines will be a matter of inquiry today. In the warehouse there was a refrigerating plant and during the fire the ammonia tanks ex-

[1] *The Chicago Tribune,* July 13, 1894, p. 5. Earlier mention of the Negro in this strike occurred when the colored people became cognizant of the fact that the American Railway Union barred the Negro from union membership. The Negroes retaliated by forming the Anti-Strikers' Railroad Union, with R. B. Stephens as president. *The Daily Inter Ocean,* July 2, 1894, p. 12.

[2] 'The expert work is being done by bosses and foremen. A few English speaking helpers with a number of Poles and negroes complete the gang. (*The Chicago Tribune,* July 15, 1894, p. 3.) 'The colored men went to work out of revenge for treatment received at the hands of the American Railway Union.' (*The Chicago Herald,* July 17, 1894, p. 8.) Papers bearing the same date as those telling of the trouble feared by the packers because of the use of colored men, carry the story of the murder of Negroes at Pratt City, Alabama, during a strike. *The Chicago Record,* July 17, 1894, p. 2; *The Chicago Tribune,* July 17, 1894, p. 1.

[3] *The Chicago Record,* July 18, 1894, p. 2; *ibid.,* July 27, p. 8. 'The crowd around the general time-keeper's office for Morris and Co. became so great that a body of militia with fixed bayonets was needed to urge the men away. . . . Poles, Bohemians and negroes predominated, but nearly all nationalities were represented.' *Ibid.,* August 3, 1894, p. 5.

[4] *Ibid.,* August 3, 1894, p. 5.

[5] *Ibid.,* July 19, 1894, p. 2.

ploded. This started an every-day dynamic scare. By the light
of the roaring flames an effigy of a negro hanging from a tele-
phone pole was brought out in relief. Across the breast a
placard was pinned with the words, "Nigger scabs" in big black
letters.[1]

Swinging from the cross-tree of a telegraph pole at the corner
of Root and Halsted Streets, near the entrance of the yards, the
effigy of a negro roustabout was suspended. A black false face
of hideous expression had been fixed upon the head of straw,
and a placard pinned upon the breast of the figure bore the
skull and cross-bones with the words "nigger scab" above and
below in bold letters. A white foreman over one of the packing
house gangs resigned his position when he was told he must
work with negroes.[2]

Early yesterday morning a number of negroes going to work
at Armour and Company's packing house were assaulted and
badly beaten.[3]

The feeling that has existed between the white and colored employees of Armour and Company has greatly increased. The
gang bosses are white men. At one time all ate in the same
room, if not at the same table, and now the colored contingent
is fed in another department. The color line has caused many
bosses to resign.[4]

Following the defeat of the workmen, the movement of
nationality groups within the packing companies and in the
vicinity of the yards continued. The Irish and Germans
no longer held a monopoly of the work, and moved farther
from the neighborhood. After 1895, Lithuanians arrived,
followed by a constant and increasing infiltration of Slovaks,
Russian Poles, Greeks, Italians and Russian Hebrews.[5]

The Negroes hired during the strike of 1894 were too few
to make an appreciable difference in the number of wage-
earners needed by the packing houses to continue operations. Their contribution was of another order; that of
keeping the workers divided and of adding conflict to a
situation in which it was already rife. Further, by this
move the packers profited on two accounts; first, they tapped

[1] The Chicago Times, July 19, 1894, p. 1; The Chicago Record, July 19,
1894, p. 1. Other newspapers of the same date deny that there was a fire.
[2] The Chicago Record, July 19, 1894, p. 2.
[3] The Chicago Herald, July 19, 1894, p. 1.
[4] Ibid., July 20, 1894, p. 8.
[5] Bulletin of the Bureau of Labor, X (1905), pp. 2-3.

an almost inexhaustible supply of cheap labor; second, they
secured thereby a labor force offering even greater resistance
to unionization, through racial antagonism, than that supplied by the immigrant through language handicap and nationality hatreds.

III

Even though employment was disagreeable, filthy, un-
healthful, degrading,[1] and the wages low, hours unregulated,
the speed intense, still the law of 'supply and demand'
brought masses of immigrants to the gates to clamor for
work.[2] Plenty was available for the 'greenhorn,' the
'hunky,' the 'sheeny.' Even the 'nigger' got a job. Finding
difficulty in procuring employment elsewhere, they were in
no position to be critical of, or to dictate, the terms under
which they worked.[3] Sixty-five per cent received an average
wage of 16 cents an hour, or $5 to $6 a week.[4] The receipt
of $1.85 a day was 'good pay'; the opportunity to work more
than 35 hours in any one week was exceptional. Gangs of
workmen were reduced and speeded-up by means of the professional pace-setter.[5]

[1] The four following references contain descriptions of the conditions of
employment in the yards from 1904 to 1917:
  a. J. B. Reynolds and C. P. Neill, 'Conditions in Chicago Stock Yards.'
     House of Representatives, Document No. 873, 1906.
  b. United States Commission on Industrial Relations, *Final Report and
     Testimony,* 1916, IV, pp. 3459-3531.
  c. *Meeting of the President's Mediation Commission and the Representatives
     of the Various Trade Unions,* and *Meeting Between the Packing Concerns
     and the President's Mediation Committee, Chicago, Illinois, December
     21-25, 1917,* pp. 1-528.
  d. *Arbitration of Wages and Hours of Labor in the Packing House Industry,*
     Hon. Samuel Alschuler, Arbitrator, Transcript of Proceedings, I-VI,
     pp. 1-4067.
[2] The percentage of various nationalities in the yards was approximately:
Americans and Scotch, about 2 per cent; Germans, 15 per cent; Irish, 25
per cent; Poles, 20 per cent; Bohemians, 20 per cent. The remaining were
Lithuanians, Slovaks, and a few Krains, and the most recent arrivals, Finns
and Greeks. *Bulletin of the Bureau of Labor,* X (1905), p. 3.
[3] The social conditions in the community are portrayed in: Charles J.
Bushnell, *The Social Problem at the Chicago Stock Yards* (Chicago: The
University of Chicago Press, 1902); E. Abbott and S. P. Breckinridge,
'Housing Conditions in Chicago, 1911, III: Back of the Yards,' *American
Journal of Sociology,* XVI, p. 433-68; Howard E. Wilson, *Mary McDowell
Neighbor* (Chicago: The University of Chicago Press, 1928), chaps. II, III,
IV.
[4] Homer D. Call, *The Chicago Chronicle.* August 1, 1904, p. 2.
[5] The 1904 strike and events leading up to it are described by J. R.
Commons, 'Labor Conditions in Meat Packing and the Recent Strike,' *Quar-
terly Journal of Economics,* XIX (1904-05), pp. 1-32.

The skilled workers, especially the German and Irish cattle butchers, were aware of the magnitude of the problem created for those who wished to identify themselves permanently with the industry. Their positions were being invaded. Insecurity lurked in every move of the packers. A day's labor was unbearably hard. Men were exhausted at the end of nine, ten, or twelve hours of continuous performance. If a man slowed down from fatigue after a few years on a killing gang, he was replaced by someone fresher and more vigorous.

As other industries in the community offered more attractive conditions of employment to experienced workers, many representatives of the older nationality groups left the packing houses. On the other hand, the hardships and adversities suffered there kindled within some the determination to 'stick' and to make their work acceptable and decent for themselves or for those workers who were to follow them. Their craft was at stake; in the industry which used it, they felt a proprietary claim. The Germans and Irish thus became famous about 'Packingtown' for dogged tenacity and defiance, as well as for skill in butchering, sausage-making, and the curing of meat.

During the opening years of the twentieth century, the workmen of 'Packingtown' came under a new influence and leadership. The Amalgamated Meat Cutters and Butcher Workmen of North America [1] sent Michael Donnelly, a master-organizer of men and women,[2] into the Chicago district. The butchers, the semi-skilled, and laborers of all ranks, blacklisted for previous union activities, were his chief allies. The timid, the fearful, the indifferent, the oppressed, the weary, were cajoled into joining his union. Any man or woman who was 'good enough' to be employed

---

[1] January, 1897, the Amalgamated Meat Cutters and Butcher Workmen of North America received its charter from the American Federation of Labor. *Report of Proceedings of the Sixth General Convention, Amalgamated Meat Cutters and Butcher Workmen of North America*, 1906, p. 10.

[2] An account of the organization of Local 183 and the effort of the women workers to function as trade-unionists may be found in the following references: Alice Henry, *The Trade Union Woman* (New York: D. Appleton and Company, 1915), pp. 52-58. John R. Commons, 'Women in Unions. Meat Packing Industry,' *American Federationist*, XIII (1906), Part I, pp. 382-83; Howard E. Wilson, *Mary McDowell Neighbor*, pp. 85-90.

in the yards was eagerly welcomed into the organization.[1] Foreign and Negro men and women were invited to join; many responded and paid their dues.

At a union meeting which I attended, a colored man was the officer who presented a group for initiation composed of four nationalities, needing interpreters in the Bohemian, Polish, Lithuanian, and German languages. The labor union has been the only institution so far that has brought the immigrant in touch with English speaking men for a common cause and is preparing them for self-government.[2]

The high purpose and perspicacity embodied in the union and finding expression in the district are said to have prevented a race feud, broken down prejudices between different nationalities, and established a real fellowship of workers. Moreover, an investigation by the United States Department of Commerce and Labor corroborated the assertion that the union was the only Americanizing influence in the stockyards for the Poles, Lithuanians, and Slavs.[3] In the words of a Lithuanian workman, not only were all the nationalities combined, but '. . . the best thing the union does is to make me feel more independent. I do not have to pay to get a job and I cannot be discharged unless I am no good.' [4]

An auspicious beginning, followed by an admirable record of achievement in dealing with the packers, marked the three years of the union's heyday in 'Packingtown.' [5] But on Tuesday, July 12, 1904, at twelve o'clock a strike [6] was

[1] See the *Official Journal*, A.M.C. and B.W. of N.A., September, 1904, p. 7.
[2] Mary McDowell, *The Chicago Daily News*, July 29, 1904, p. 3.
[3] *Bulletin*, X (1905), p. 4.
[4] Antanas Kaztauskis, 'From Lithuania to the Chicago Stockyards,' *Independent*, LVII (1904), p. 248.
[5] The union strove for uniformity of employment conditions, hours of work, and wages among the workers in the various packing centers. Among its gains were the following: it remedied one of the greatest causes of complaint, the irregularity of hours, and secured four legal holidays for all workers. The 'contract' which had been enforced following the strike of 1886 was abolished. The cattle and sheep butchers' unions put into operation a 'scale of work' by which output was limited. The former adopted a plan of promotion and seniority. Verbal agreements were the rule, each local union acting autonomously. The three butchers' unions effected gratifying agreements, the unskilled took what they could get.
[6] The immediate cause of the strike lay in the union demand for an agreement to include the same pay and conditions of work in all the packing

hastily and blunderingly launched.[1] Nor did the union leaders retrieve the colossal error which involved so many working men and women and had as its accompaniments hardship, bitterness, and untold sufferings, loss of life and property; they matched, or rather transcended it, by calling, after a two-day cessation of hostilities,[2] the 'second strike' of the summer on July 22.[3]

In 1904, the union struck to establish a uniform wage rate for the unskilled, hoping thereby to maintain the wage scale already gained for the skilled laborers. Leaders of organized labor announced that they struck to defend the under-dog, the rights of the man lowest and least protected in the industry.[4] These were chiefly the foreign laborers, who constituted 25 per cent of all workers and were paid less than 20 cents an hour. But ironically enough the strike-breakers who eagerly manned the plants, replacing the organized workers and enabling the packers to carry on operations without reëmploying the strikers, were none other than the common laborers—Negroes, Greeks, Slavs, and Lithuanians—for whose sake the strike had been called. As newcomers and individuals, free of class and industrial consciousness in a new contingency, ignorant of a trade and the factors in an industrial situation, they were willing to accept work under almost any conditions or circumstances. Quan-

centers, and more especially an 18 cent minimum wage rate for the unskilled. *Report of Proceedings of the Sixth General Convention*, A.M.C. and B.W. of N.A., 1906, pp. 7-20.

[1] Statements by the packers and the union on the calling of the strike may be found in the following: *The Chicago Daily Tribune*, August 22, 1904, pp. 1, 5; *ibid.*, August 23, 1904, p. 3; *Report of Proceedings of the Sixth General Convention*, 1906, pp. 7-9.

[2] The allied trades, affiliated with the Packing Trades Council, joined the second strike which became effective after the Council was joined by the teamsters on July 27. The existence of a Mechanical Trades Council furnished a divisive factor which was overcome in 1918 by the formation of a Stock Yards Labor Council, and a federated form of organization.

[3] *The Chicago Daily Tribune*, September 10, 1904, p. 1; Call, *Proceedings of the Sixth General Convention*, pp. 8-9, 20. *The Chicago Record-Herald*, July 22, 1904, p. 5; July 23, 1904, pp. 1-2; July 24, 1904, pp. 1-2; *Official Journal*, August, 1904, p. 24.

[4] '. . . Shall the standard of the most poorly paid workers of Europe be established by the packers as the standard of life for American citizens? Shall labor be treated as a mere expense item, or shall it be treated as a sharer in the profits of industry? . . . This is the real issue in the contest in which the butcher workmen are engaged. We leave the public to judge whether right is not on our side.' Executive Board of A.M.C. and B.W. of N.A., by Homer D. Call, Secretary, *The Inter Ocean*, August 1, 1904, p. 2.

tity rather than quality of workers became the more serious consideration and the issue upon which the termination of the strike depended. Division of labor, standardization and simplification of processes, and a cheap, plentiful supply of immigrants were now the allies of the packers, who were in a position to utilize advantageously large numbers of workmen possessing little or no experience.

After the orderly exit of the workers,[1] Negro strike-breakers were smuggled into the yards on July 12. The pickets left their posts as midnight approached. Twelve policemen then escorted fifty Negroes to the beef house of Nelson Morris and Company, where they were lodged. The agent who collected them at Thirty-Fifth Street and Armour Avenue received one dollar a head. During the next two weeks, trainloads of several hundred Negroes, accompanied by officers of the law, arrived daily.[2] Italian and Greek strike-breakers were reported not less frequently. After successfully eluding the pickets for a day, a 'phantom train' of several hundred immigrants from Ellis Island pulled into the yards. There was no mistaking the immigrants loaded as they were with boxes and bundles bearing the fresh stamp of the custom-house. Peasants from southern Europe were shipped from the port of entry to jobs awaiting them in the great Middle West. Their first homes in the land of opportunity were in hog-killing houses and lard refineries.[3]

The rôle of the Negro in the strike of 1904 differed from that which he had assumed in 1894. He was the center of attack from the moment the strike broke. The race now provided a sufficient number of workmen to man countless detailed jobs for which no training was required. But more than this, colored men and women were successful in gaining employment as scabs because of the stolid opposition with which the majority of them, thus adding to the bitterness created by their presence, met trade-unionism. As the presence of an increasing number of immigrants and Negroes

[1] The Chicago Daily Tribune, July 13, 1904, p. 2.
[2] Ibid., July 25, 1904, p. 2; ibid., July 26, 1904, p. 2; The Inter Ocean, July 30, 1904, p. 2.
[3] The Chicago Daily News, August 4, 1904, p. 1.

in the yards indicated the success of the packers in resuming operations, racial antipathies and hatreds were kindled. To the striking union men no scabs were as loathsome as the Negroes who took their jobs. Easily distinguishable, they were conspicuous among the strike-breakers and suffered the animus which is vented upon all scabs. They were jeered, if they emerged from the plants under police escort; chased and attacked, if alone.[1] Pistol shots invariably brought the assaults to a close. Among the first of the strike-breakers to be hired, they were among the first to be asked to leave at the conclusion of hostilities.

Twenty-five per cent of the strike-breakers, including many Negroes, were lodged in the packing houses for three weeks.[2] Smallpox appeared: it was known that the services of four physicians were required for vaccination; that the patients had been removed to a pesthouse;[3] that blank death certificates had been furnished the packers.[4] Fire broke out in buildings used for lodgings.[5] In one of the Swift buildings mattresses were stretched along the floor. In another there were tiers of bunks four rows high. 'They did not look very inviting, but the negroes who occupy them appear

[1] *The Chicago Daily Tribune*, July 16, 1904, p. 2; *The Sunday Record-Herald*, Chicago, July 24, 1904, p. 2; *The Chicago Record-Herald*, July 27, 1904, p. 2; *ibid.*, August 21, 1904, p. 4; *The Chicago Daily News*, August 25, 1904, p. 2.

[2] The housing of the strike-breakers was not effected without opposition. The union complained to the city of the physical and moral conditions under which lodgings were provided. The City Health Department examined the plants and the sleeping-quarters and was satisfied. A few days later both the union and the packers requested Mayor Harrison to conduct a second investigation. The insurance companies became agitated. The result of a survey by Health Commissioner Reynolds and Building Commissioner Williams was submitted to Corporation Counsel Tolman, who ruled that Section 65 of the Building Ordinance was being violated. The packers now appealed for an injunction against the city officials' interference with the housing of employees. Judge Brentano granted the injunction. *The Chicago Daily Tribune*, August 4, 1904, p. 2; *ibid.*, August 9, 1904, p. 1; *ibid.*, August 10, 1904, p. 2; *ibid.*, August 11, 1904, p. 3; *ibid.*, August 12, 1904, p. 3; *The Sunday Tribune*, August 14, 1904, Part I, p. 1; *The Chicago Daily Tribune*, August 16, 1904, p. 1; *ibid.*, August 20, 1904, p. 1; *The Sunday Tribune*, August 21, 1904, Part I, p. 3; *The Chicago Daily Tribune*, August 22, 1904, p. 5; *ibid.*, August 23, 1904, p. 3; *ibid.*, August 24, 1904, p. 3; *ibid.*, August 25, 1904, p. 3; *The Chicago Daily News*, August 16, 1904, p. 2; *ibid.*, August 24, 1904, p. 1.

[3] *The Chicago Evening Post*, August 8, 1904, p. 2.

[4] 'John Fitzpatrick . . . said that the packers were supplied with blank burial permits which enabled them to ship the bodies of men killed in the plants out of the city without investigation by the police or coroner.' *The Chicago Sunday Tribune*, August 21, 1904, Part I, p. 3.

[5] *The Chicago Daily Tribune*, August 25, 1904, p. 3.

to be happy.'[1]   Physical and moral conditions in the 'scab hatcheries' became questionable.[2]

A great deal has been made of the immoral practices which were said to have been prevalent[3] and the Negroes' part in them.   Certainly the setting was conducive to moral laxity, but the press doubtless exaggerated the state of affairs in the interest of a lurid story.   On the other hand, fights over women and crap games, guns pulled in the heat of gambling or a drunken brawl, seem to have been the common record of almost any day.[4]   Efforts were made to relieve the monotony of the strike-breakers' exile by excursions to the Black Belt over the week-end,[5] but the coaches provided were always insufficient in number.   Moreover, many of the workers had no place to go in a strange city, and preferred to 'hang about,' loaf, or 'make merry' in the rambling hallways, sheds, and buildings of the packing companies, or loiter and visit among the cattle-pens.[6]

The union made a last desperate effort to curb the influx of the Negroes without whom the packers would have had greater difficulty in winning the strike.[7]   It appealed directly

[1] *The Inter Ocean,* July 30, 1904, p. 2.

[2] 'Each carrying a small lard pail containing water for morning ablutions, 348 men last night climbed the narrow stairway to the sleeping quarters on the third floor.   Every floor and the walls are saturated with grease, and the danger of fire was evident.   The sleeping room is about 200 feet long, sixty feet wide, with a ceiling, the roof, about eight feet high.   There are no cots, only long rows of latticing across which are dirty mattresses, each with a soiled pillow, both devoid of linen, and a dirty blue blanket.   Some of the men disrobed, others retained their clothing, but all, putting their water pails under the lattice, piled into bed.   The ventilation is comparatively good, but the smell of lard is almost stifling.'   *The Chicago Daily News,* August 23, 1904, p. 2.

[3] 'Then the homes of the nation's meat supply were turned into infernos of hells, where the devil and his imp shot craps with the harlot and the prostitute in the packers' stockade.   An orgy of ghoulishness was permitted in all packing centers—an orgy which would have made the Angel Gabriel break the note of his horn if he were inclined to blow.'   Cornelius J. Hayes, *The Butcher Workman,* July, 1921, p. 7.

[4] *The Chicago Daily Tribune,* August 29, 1904, p. 3.

[5] *The Chicago Evening Post,* August 8, 1904, p. 1.

[6] *The Chicago Sunday Tribune,* August 14, 1904, p. 3.   'While three negro preachers held services in one packing house, seven poker tables were in operation on the floor below.'   *The Inter Ocean,* August 1, 1904, p. 2.

[7] Without the colored men and women now employed in the plants,' said John Fitzpatrick, organizer for the Chicago Federation of Labor, 'the companies would not be able to operate.   The employers have been unable to hire white men.   If the present system is kept up, race hatred will be stirred up and trouble may follow.'   *The Chicago Daily Tribune,* August 24, 1904, p. 3.

to the leader of the Negro race, Booker T. Washington, at Tuskegee, asking him to interpret the situation to his people.

> Organized labor in Chicago representing 250,000 men and women of all races, respectfully requests you to address a mass meeting of colored people in this city on the subject: "Should negroes become strike-breakers?" Organized labor for years has endeavored to overcome race hatred, and the fact that hundreds of negroes are acting as strike-breakers to aid the beef trust to reduce wages is undoing all of the good work done in years along that line.[1]
>
> (Signed) JOHN FITZPATRICK and W. M. ROSSELL,
> of the committee.

Mr. Washington's private secretary telegraphed regrets that other plans interfered with Mr. Washington's acceptance.[2] At the close of the struggle,[3] workers who had participated in bread and meat riots stampeded the hiring stations. A small majority of the colored workmen retained their positions, many were 'let out,' while a third group was intimidated and warned that it would be unwise to remain in the yards' vicinity. The Negroes who endeavored to remain in the employ of the packers were challenged and attacked by the returning union men. By this method the shrinkage in the percentage of Negro workmen was accelerated. Within three or four days lodgings in the yards were discontinued. The colored deserters were herded into special trains which carried them to the Black Belt. The packers preferred white laborers and hired them to replace the Negroes whose services as strike-breakers were no longer required.

[1] *The Chicago Daily Tribune*, August 24, 1904, p. 3.
[2] *Ibid.*, August 26, 1904, p. 3.
[3] The agreement signed by the packers and the A.M.C. and B.W. of N.A. may be found in the *Proceedings of the Sixth General Convention*, 1906, pp. 9-10.

CHAPTER III

THE NEGRO AND TRADE-UNIONISM

THE influx of Negroes into the yards, which began during the 1904 strike, was never entirely stopped. From 1917 to 1921, Negro workmen found their status enhanced because as members of a distinct racial group they were the men without whom the packers could not continue production and at the same time ignore the demands of organized labor. Nor could organized labor afford to ignore them longer. At each succeeding crisis in the events of four years which terminated in the strike of December, 1921, and January, 1922, the contending parties recognized increasingly that the final outcome would in large measure be determined by the colored men. The more critical exigencies which affected the rôle of the Negro were: first, the renewed activity of the Amalgamated Meat Cutters and Butcher Workmen of North America, organizing all workers in the stockyards, and terminating in a period of federal administration of labor on the basis of an agreement signed between the packers and the Government on one side, and the unions and the Government on the other; second, the signing of a second agreement and the subsequent membership drive; third, the formation of District Council No. 9 and the Chicago race riots which put an end to the campaign to increase union membership; fourth, the concluding six months' agreement and the final drive for union adherents; and fifth, the strike of 1921 and the introduction of employee representation plans.

Organizing the 'Unorganizable'

When, during the World War the Government asked the packers to furnish one thousand carloads of meat a day,[1] the Amalgamated Meat Cutters and Butcher Workmen of North America realized the unprecedented opportunity to regain a foothold in the Chicago establishments, and in-

[1] *Meeting of the President's Mediation Commission*, p. 120.

augurated its second organization drive.[1]   The Stock Yards
Labor Council was formed on July 25, 1917, under the
jurisdiction of the Chicago Federation of Labor.   John
Fitzpatrick, William Z. Foster, and John Johnstone, constituting the spearhead of an aggressive phalanx, were the
organizers in the yards.   Their success was no less marked
than that of the 'intrepid Mike,' in 1904.[2]   By November,
they had swept aside the packers' opposition to trade-union
membership, created widespread disregard for the employers' cajolery in the form of increase in wages and improvement in working conditions,[3] and overcome the fear
of spies.   The union, which boasted 100 per cent organization of the skilled workers, 90 per cent of all workers and a
membership between 35,000 and 40,000 in Chicago, felt
itself firmly intrenched in the industry.[4]
    The campaign was effective not only because the unions

---

[1] In Chicago, the A.M.C. and B.W. of N.A. was almost extinct from
1904 to 1916. The defeat of the 1904 strike had brought a dissolution of
the union and demoralization of the blacklisted workmen. For twelve years
the packers made agreements only with the Teamsters' Union and the Hair-
spinners' Union. John Fitzpatrick, *Meeting of the President's Mediation Commission*, pp. 11-12.

[2] On September 9, 1917, aided by the American Federation of Labor, the most
gigantic and spectacular campaign for union members in the history of the
industry was launched. Before its close it had become national in scope.
Although a discrepancy occurs in the figures issued by the union, it is
conceded that in July, 1917, the total membership in the union was 6,500;
January, 1918, the membership numbered 100,000, and about 125 charters
had been granted to new locals. Within eighteen months the deficit had been
removed, and a surplus of $100,000 accumulated. *Report of Proceedings of
the Ninth General Convention*, A.M.C. and B.W. of N.A., 1917, pp. 120, 143;
The Butcher Workman, March, 1919, p. 1; *ibid.*, May, 1918, p. 1; *ibid.*,
November, 1919, pp. 1, 2.

[3] John Fitzpatrick, *Meeting of the President's Mediation Commission*, pp. 12,
440. Between 1904 and 1916 labor was ruled with a 'mailed fist.' No wage
increases were conceded until 1916, when 2½-cent increases were offered each
time organization was attempted. In November, 1917, a 5 cent wage increase
was offered which was withdrawn when its futility in preventing an increase
in union membership was realized. (John E. O'Hern, *ibid.*, p. 272.) Four
increases in wages were given to the workers from June, 1916, to December,
1917. The unskilled workers and the women were the chief beneficiaries.
(John F. Hart, *Report of Proceedings of the Ninth General Convention*, 1917,
p. 29). An increase in wages of more than $6,000,000 a year was attributed
to the success in organizing workers in all the large centers in which the industry was located. (Judge Samuel Alschuler, United States Bureau of Labor
Statistics, *Monthly Review*, May, 1918, VI, No. V, p. 116.) A raise in pay,
March, 1916, operated to equalize the wages of common labor who thereafter
were paid 20 cents an hour. The subsequent raises in the hourly pay of all
employees were: October, 1916, 2½ cents; April, 1917, 2½ cents; September,
1917, 2½ cents. In addition to their piece-work wages, piece-workers were given
this hourly wage for the time employed.

[4] *Meeting of the President's Mediation Commission*, p. 25.

adopted a federated form which enabled them to coöperate and to present a united front, but also because of their ability to organize the unskilled workers, who presented an even greater obstacle to unionism than they had on previous occasions. A cardinal principle of the campaign was that the unskilled workmen, the lowest in the scale of employment, and the most recent to enter the industry, a large proportion of whom were foreign-born [1] and a second formidable group, Negro, could not be permanently benefited by the altruistic and philanthropic efforts of the skilled. The resistance of the foreign-born, who had been pronounced 'unorganizable,' was overcome and their suspicions allayed by representatives of their own nationalities, chief among whom was the powerful, domineering, and indefatigable John Kikulski.[2] With his 'loud voice and ha ha laugh,' and his fiery, impassioned oratory, he pictured a 'brighter day with more pay' for all workers. The big Polish local, No. 554, strove, by proclaiming its jurisdiction over all workers who spoke a Slavic language, to outdistance in membership every group in the council, and to set up its leader as the indisputable and final authority.

Almost twelve thousand Negroes were now working for the packers, the number increasing in direct ratio to the success of the unions in organizing the white laborers. Not only were the colored workmen regarded as being almost immune to organization and unreliable after joining, but the unions were uncertain as to the limits to which they wished to carry their Jim Crow tactics. A few unions of skilled workers admitted Negroes; [3] the majority of those

---

[1] Poles, Austrians, and Lithuanians performed most of the unskilled work and predominated among the nationalities, which numbered about thirty-one. (*Meeting of the President's Mediation Commission*, p. 228.) In 1917, it was reported that in the packing centers of the United States the nationality distribution of workers was as follows: American-born, white, 24 per cent; colored, 20 per cent; Poles, 17 per cent; Austrians, about 10 per cent; Lithuanians, 12 per cent; Germans, 5 per cent; Russians, 5 per cent; English, Irish, Scotch, Canadian, 5 per cent; miscellaneous, 2 per cent. John E. O'Hern, *Meeting of the President's Mediation Commission*, p. 228.

[2] Statements in regard to the work and character of John Kikulski, organizer, Martin Murphy, president, J. W. Johnstone. secretary-treasurer of the Stock Yards Labor Council, which were issued by Dennis Lane, secretary-treasurer of the A.M.C. and B.W. of N.A., appear in *The Butcher Workman*, November, 1919, pp. 2, 5.

[3] *Meeting of the President's Mediation Commission*, p. 106.

in the Stock Yards Labor Council, which included about twenty unions, drew the color line sharply. Although the success of the colored men in helping to defeat the previous strike gained a place for them among union 'considerations and problems,' unanimity of opinion as to how to solve the racial problem did not exist. Following the example set by Michael Donnelly in 1904, some urged that the colored man should be admitted to the existing unions. Although constitutional provisions in some instances prohibited this, debarment came, not from legislative action or precept, but from the dictates of racial prejudice and animosity. Samuel Gompers, president of the American Federation of Labor, to whom the predicament was referred, 'solved' it by granting permission to create separate unions to which Negroes were admitted. This also partially met the Negro's distrust of organizations governed by white officers in which he constituted a minority. In the absence of objection from the international unions which barred colored workers from membership, Negroes were affiliated through the authorization of special charters.[1]

[1] In 1881, at its inception, the Federation of Organized Trades and Labor Unions which later became the American Federation of Labor, followed the tradition and policy of its predecessors, the National Labor Union and the Knights of Labor, in regard to the desirability of including workers of all creeds, colors, and nationalities in its membership. A colored delegate was in attendance at the first convention. (*Report of the First Annual Session of the Federation of Organized Trades and Labor Unions of the United States and Canada,* held in Pittsburgh, Pennsylvania, December 15, 16, 17, 18, 1881; reprinted in 1906, p. 16; E. E. Wolfe, *Admission to American Trade Unions,* Baltimore: The Johns Hopkins Press, 1912, Johns Hopkins University Studies in Historical and Political Science, Series XXX, No. III, pp. 113-16.)   In 1893, a resolution was unanimously adopted reaffirming 'as one of the cardinal principles of the labor movement that the working people must unite and organize, irrespective of creed, color, sex, nationality or politics.' (*Report of Proceedings of the Thirteenth Annual Convention,* A. F. of L., held at Chicago, Illinois, December 11 to 19, inclusive, 1893; reprinted in 1905, p. 56.)   In 1894, a similar resolution was adopted (*Report of Proceedings of the Fourteenth Annual Convention,* A. F. of L., held at Denver, Colorado, December 11, 12, 13, 14, 15, 16, 17, 18, 1894; reprinted in 1905, p. 25), and again it was reaffirmed in 1897, but without the unanimous approval of the convention. On the latter occasion the resolution was introduced in order to denounce as untrue the statement of Mr. Booker T. Washington, that the trade-unions were placing obstacles in the way of the material advancement of the Negro. (*Report of Proceedings of the Seventeenth Annual Convention,* A. F. of L., held at Nashville, Tennessee, December 13 to 21, inclusive, 1897; reprinted in 1905, pp. 78-79.)   An important recommendation was passed in 1900 which provided that 'Separate charters may be issued to Central Labor Unions, Local Unions, or Federal Labor Unions, composed exclusively of colored members, where, in the judgment of the Executive Council it appears advisable to do so.' (*Report of Proceedings of the Twentieth Annual Convention,* A. F.

Two colored organizers, Messrs. Bell and Robinson, whose services were donated for several years by the Illinois Miners, were put into the field.[1] But no sooner was Local 651, to which white workmen were also admitted and in which the majority of the Negroes were enrolled,[2] chartered than the cry of 'Jim Crow' was raised. The outstanding complaint of discrimination raised by the colored workmen arose from the fact that in joining Local 651, wage-earners of all trades—mechanics, plumbers, and the like—received membership cards in a butchers' union and that this membership was recognized only within the establishments located in the Union Stock Yards. To meet this dilemma the interchangeability of membership in all locals affiliated with the Amalgamated Meat Cutters and Butcher Workmen of North America was proclaimed.[3] The fact was not concealed that without the Negroes the yards could not be unionized. The inclusion of colored workers in the packing industry unions was a sincere, albeit calculating, gesture from organized

of L., held at Louisville, Kentucky, December 6 to 15, inclusive, 1900; reprinted in 1905, p. 129.) In 1910, the convention unanimously reaffirmed the position of the Federation which was taken in 1897 and the constitutional addition of 1900. (*Report of Proceedings of the Thirtieth Annual Convention*, A. F. of L., held at St. Louis, Missouri, November 14 to 26, inclusive, 1910, pp. 237, 333-34.) In 1917, and in 1918, the conventions stressed the necessity of organizing the colored man. (*Report of Proceedings of the Thirty-Seventh Annual Convention*, A. F. of L., held at Buffalo, New York, November 12-24, 1917, p. 350; *Report of Proceedings of the Thirty-Eighth Annual Convention*, held at St. Paul, Minnesota, June 10 to 20, inclusive, 1918, pp. 130-31, 198-99, 205, 263-64.) The 1919 convention had five separate resolutions presented to it by the colored delegates. The following recommendation was unanimously approved: that 'Many international unions affiliated with the American Federation of Labor admit colored workers to membership, and in so doing protect their rights and interests. Other organizations affiliated with the American Federation of Labor refuse admittance to colored workers, which brings about the present complaints. In such cases your committee recommends that the American Federation of Labor organize these colored workers under charters from the American Federation of Labor.' *Report of Proceedings of the Thirty-Ninth Annual Convention*, A. F. of L., held at Atlantic City, New Jersey, June 9 to 23, inclusive, 1919, pp. 304-06.

[1] John Walker, *Meetings of the President's Mediation Commission*, pp. 136-37. The American Federation of Labor considered the appointment of colored organizers beginning with the year 1893, but for financial reasons none was added to the staff. (*Report of Proceedings*, A. F. of L., 1893, p. 40.) The first salaried colored officer was appointed in 1904.

[2] Among the men who served Local 651 in an official capacity the following were prominent: Henry Sherfie, Theodore Payne, George W. Downing, A. K. Foote, James P. Brown.

[3] William Z. Foster, *The Great Strike and Its Lessons* (New York: B. W. Huebsch, Inc., 1920), pp. 211-12; The Chicago Commission on Race Relations, *The Negro in Chicago*, (The University of Chicago Press, 1922); pp. 428-29.

labor. Necessity demanded that recognition be given to the strength of the Negro group; expediency dictated the membership policy.

Capable colored organizers were not easy to secure; after several disappointments in hiring men who proved hostile to the labor movement, the services of Mr. I. H. Bratton and Mr. George Strather were obtained. They were assisted by Mr. John Riley from the American Federation of Labor.[1] Ninety per cent of the colored stockyard workers joined unions, the percentage being higher for northern Negroes.[2] Over-optimism as to the results of the creation of separate colored unions was quickly dissipated. The Negro was accused of being a better 'joiner,' although 'none too good,' than an active or intelligent union member. If he took the trouble to attend the meeting of his local, he was inert and unintelligent or over-zealous in the discussion of trifling and inconsequential details. Only the colored man who was ambitious, who was beginning to compete as an individual with a white man for a semi-skilled or skilled position in the industry, was persuaded of the advantages to be gained by standing with his fellow workmen. Interest in a movement sponsored by white workmen was difficult to secure.

No less alert than the unions in recognizing the importance of the unskilled workmen, and in particular the unique position held by the Negro, the packers tried to thwart the unions and limit their success by employing more colored wage-earners. On previous occasions, when confronted with the menace of union organization, they had become convinced that 'hungry Negroes were a bulwark against it.' Colored men were encouraged to come to the yards; their numbers in the industry were increased. The following telegram and letter, signed by an associate of the General Superintendent of Swift and Company, which was taken from the Denver files by the Federal Trade Commission, demon-

---

[1] The Amalgamated Meat Cutters and Butcher Workmen of North America employed two additional colored organizers, Mr. George Reed, who was assigned to Kansas City, and Mr. C. Ford to St. Louis. The Negro organizers were sent to Oklahoma City and Fort Worth, Texas, to spread the trade-union gospel among the southern colored workers. They were hired at a salary of $54 a week, which was later reduced to $42. Both this rate of pay and the reduction were in line with the amounts paid to all organizers.

[2] Dennis Lane, *Meeting of the President's Mediation Commission*, p. 105.

strates the activity and the policy of the company in this respect:

Swift & Co., Denver File, Chicago, July 11, 1917.   Swift & Co., #16 USY, Denver, Colo.   (Translation.)   Answering: Want you to work closely with Hanson to prevent your house becoming organized, handling so as not to force a strike.   Advise find cause other than being members labor unions for dropping two men mentioned or other active members and dispense with services as soon as practicable.   Arranging have Mr. Jackson your house Thursday.   Keep us fully posted.   J. Burns.

Letter from Swift & Co., Denver File, Swift and Company, Stock Yards Station, Denver, Colo., August 28, 1917; Mr. Louis F. Swift, President, Swift & Co., Stock Yards, Chicago.   Dear Sir: Answering your letter of the 21st, regarding colored help at the Denver plant, we have recently started an Employment Bureau at the plant which will handle matters of this kind and we shall start at once to increase the percentage of colored help in the plant with the intention of getting it to 15 per cent or higher as soon as we possibly can.   Yours respectfully, Swift & Co., per J. B. Manager's Office.[1]

Union leaders came to feel that the packers were taking the initiative in creating racial friction and antagonism between the colored and the white worker in order to keep their employees divided.   The rate of discharge was high among white union members, and continued to rise following an increase in the ranks of organized labor.   Complaint of the frequent discharges, which were often pronounced 'unwarranted,[2] carried with it a more subtle charge, for not uncommonly the place of the dismissed workman was immediately filled by a colored man.[3]

Another problem that is a very serious matter there in regard to unrest is the discharge or laying off of good competent men because they are inclined to be men that would speak for their rights at times when some employee that had formerly been

[1] *Arbitration of Wages and Hours of Labor in the Packing Industry*, IV, pp. 2303-04.   These communications were among those introduced by Frank P. Walsh during the arbitration hearings to show the attitude of the packers toward organized labor and protective legislation and their activity in employing legislative agents.
[2] *The Packinghouse Worker*, October 18, 1919, p. 1.
[3] John Kikulski, *President's Mediation Commission*, p. 133.

employed as a strike-breaker wanted a position and one of these
other men would have to make way for him, and in many cases
a white man would be laid off and a negro put in his place.
There are many positions where there are two or more men
working at some task, such as chopping hogs on a block on the
cutting floor, and they will put a big burly negro on one side
and a white man on the other, and let them battle it out for
supremacy; that is their method of arriving at efficiency.[1]

The packers made use of such agents and 'soldiers of
fortune' as Mr. Richard Parker, who advertised himself
as 'the man who was always with his race right or wrong.'
So interested in Negroes was this organizer, newspaper
editor, employment secretary, and promoter of the Race
Publishing Company, that in 1916 he distributed about
twenty thousand handbills warning workers not to join the
white man's union. His boast was that he brought more
Negroes from the South than any one man in Chicago. A
card from him constituted an open sesame to the beef and
steel companies. The migrants were warned that employment would be forfeited if they joined any save his union.
On March 10, 1917, during the period of his activities, the
'American Unity Labor Union' made its début. In May,
1920, the 'American Unity Packers' Union' was organized,
exclusively for stockyard workers. Solicitations for the
'union' occurred within the plants, the agent frequently
standing beside the time-keeper's office. A membership card
claimed to entitle its holder to work in any of the plants
of the 'Big Five.' No preliminary dues were collected by
the agent as a requisite for membership, but as the proprie-
tor of a 'race employment agency' his financial returns
from his clients were by no means negligible. A Negro organization and agency were thus created which boasted freedom from racial barriers, financial obligation, and the fear
of summary dismissal. The services rendered the packers
were two: their labor force was augmented by colored workmen, and trade-unionism became a confused issue to the
uninformed colored laborer who was unable to differentiate
between the competing legitimate and 'yellow' organiza-

[1] United States Commission on Industrial Relations, *Final Report and Testimony*, 1916, IV, p. 3518.

tions soliciting his favor.   In his own paper, the *Chicago Advocate,* the following advertisement was regularly inserted: [1]

Join the Meat Cutters and Packers Union at the stock yards, the only colored labor union at the yards. We are recognized by the packers the same as any other union and have a great number of men working there now, and if you are working in the packing plant at any trade or common labor, you can get a union card at The American Labor Union and if you are out of a job join our organization and we will help you.

Steel mills, foundries, and metal workers, railroads, shops and factories can now join one of the largest colored Union in the above plants by getting a card from your own race union where you are sure to get a square deal and we will use our organization to keep you working in these plants. The day has come when you must join some organization to get a job and keep one after you get it, and if you are not in a union you can join at our office.

A statement made in 1917 concerning the Negroes as the most recent employees in the stockyards is quoted:

The packers say that they are going to deal with their own employees. Now, then, when you come to that situation the Packers have exhausted every nationality, so far as the employees in the Stock Yards are concerned, and just as soon as any nationality developed sufficient intelligence to understand what was being done to them there, they undertake to get redress for their grievances, or get some consideration, as soon as they have accomplished that, that nationality has been ousted; then another nationality is brought in and used, and in turn they are exhausted and thrown out and another one, and so on, until they got down to,—well, the very lowest. Then the Hungarians, and others, in the Stock Yards there, I think that is about as far as they can go in that direction. Finding that they cannot get the ignorant labor which they want to deal with, they have gone to the South and brought up the negroes, brought them up here by the thousands and put them into the Stock Yards.

If we were dealing with what we call the "Northern Negro," we would not have very much difficulty, because they understand

[1] See *The Negro in Chicago,* p. 423.

the necessity of organization, and they are organized and a part of our organization, but the Southern negro is different. We figure that his slavery days ended at about the time that he came up here to work in the Packing houses. That is the kind of labor that the Stock Yards has in there now. Then the Packers say to us that they are going to deal with their own employees . . . they are going to deal with these hopeless, oppressed, and discouraged negroes, and others, that they have in there, and that means this: It means that they are going to undertake to set the standards of Labor in the packing industry by their power and their ability to deal with a class of labor that is ignorant.[1]

The Period of Federal Administration of Labor.

During 1917 union strength and authority increased. As the organized workers were unable to secure a direct agreement with the employers, a strike seemed imminent. Since this would have curtailed the food supplies of the allied armies, the President's Mediation Commission intervened, and separate agreements [2] were signed by the employers and by the union representatives on December 24 and 25.[3]

With the opening of the arbitration hearings on January 2, 1918,[4] difficulties arose, owing to differences in the two contracts, of which the signers had been unaware, and to disparity in the constructions being placed upon them.[5] Counsels for the packers and workers went into conference

[1] Fitzpatrick, *Meeting of the President's Mediation Commission*, pp. 38-40.
[2] The agreement signed by the President's Mediation Commission and the packers appears in *Meeting of the President's Mediation Commission*, pp. 423-30; that signed by the Commission and the unions is printed in *The Butcher Workman*, January, 1918, p. 2, and in the Illinois State Federation of Labor *Weekly News Letter*, December 29, 1917, pp. 1-2.
[3] The steps taken in 1917 leading to the agreements are described in *The Butcher Workman*, March, 1921, p. 4.
[4] Mr. Frank P. Walsh became counsel for the Butcher Workmen on this date and served without fee throughout the first arbitration proceedings. His aid was requested when it became evident that the packers were to be represented by attorneys. His plea for the workers at the close of the hearing, is printed in *The Butcher Workman*, March, 1918, pp. 1, 3, 4.
[5] The union thought that it had committed itself to an 'agreement for arbitration,' while the packers interpreted their pact as one not committing them to arbitration either in respect to the term specified, or in other grievances. They saw no distinction between arbitration and mediation; their understanding was that each side should come to the arbitrator and state its case and a decision should be rendered. *Meeting of the President's Mediation Commission*, pp. 419-20, 519-20. *Arbitration of Wages and Hours*, VI, pp. 3971, 3974-75.

in an effort to bring about an understanding and to effect
a settlement, but were unsuccessful.[1]

On January 17, 1918, a workers' committee [2] went to
Washington to urge the Government to take over the packing plants for the duration of the War. The packers were
summoned and met their workmen under the chairmanship
of Secretary of Labor Wilson.[3] Twelve points were agreed
upon to govern the packers and their employees in their
working relationships.[4] Six additional disputed questions
were formulated as a basis for arbitration.

Early in February, 1918, the National Council of Defense
appointed Judge Samuel S. Alschuler, of the United States
Circuit Court of Appeals, arbitrator of differences arising
in the slaughtering and meat-packing industry. On February 11, the Judge opened proceedings in the Federal Building at Chicago; these lasted until March 7 [5] and on the
thirtieth he handed down his first award.[6] Before this man
of highest judicial discretion and integrity, tempered with
human sympathy and understanding, the workers told of

[1] Mr. John Williams, who was· the first arbitrator, resigned, ostensibly because
of poor health. A dissimilarity in the two agreements existed in respect to
the appointment of a new administrator, the union holding the position of disadvantage. Both documents provided for the appointment of an administrator
by the Secretary of Labor, with the approval of the National Council of
Defense in the event of Mr. Williams' failure or inability to act. According
to the agreement signed by the union, however, the appointment was to be
made after 'consultation with the unions and employers'; according to the
agreement signed by the packers, upon 'consultation and approval with the
employers and employees.' *Arbitration of Wages and Hours,* VI, p. 3979.

[2] Among the sixteen members of the delegation was Joseph Bell, who offi-
cially represented the colored workmen in Local 651. *The Butcher Workman,*
January, 1918, pp. 1-2.

[3] *Ibid.,* March, 1918, p. 4.

[4] The eighteen 'demands' of the union were formulated on November 11 and
12, 1917, at the general convention of the Amalgamated Meat Cutters and
Butcher Workmen of North America. The first six became the basis for
the arbitration proceedings; the last twelve for the terms agreed to in joint
conference. The twelve points were settled by a committee composed of
Carl Meyer and J. G. Condon, attorneys, who represented the employers, John
Fitzpatrick and Frank P. Walsh, who represented the workers. The terms
of the agreement and the six points constituting the basis for the arbitration
proceedings are printed in *The Butcher Workman,* January, 1918, p. 1.

[5] The hearings are contained in *Arbitration of Wages and Hours of Labor in
the Packing-House Industry,* I-VI, pp. 1-4067.

[6] The credit for the victory which the award commemorated was given to
Mr. Frank P. Walsh under whose guidance it was secured. (Hart, *Report of
Proceedings of the Tenth General Convention,* A.M.C. and B.W. of N.A.,
1920, p. 85.) Mr. Walsh, however, never failed, when opportunity afforded,
to laud the leadership of John Fitzpatrick. *The Butcher Workman,* March,
1919, pp. 1, 3, 4.

privations suffered at the hands of the packers. Brought
to the stand the packers in turn laid their case before the
Judge. They, no less than the workers, became reassured
as to the qualifications of the man who held this position
of responsibility.[1]

Under the award of March 30, and the agreement arrived
at through committee action, the packing industry embodied, in this period of war-time emergency, the most
progressive standards laid down by both the Government
and the trade-unions.[2] From time to time additional grievances and matters which needed adjustment came to Judge
Alschuler [3] who served as mediator for about three and one-
half years, carrying this work in addition to that incumbent
upon him as a Federal Judge. Within a short time he became a veritable technician in the meat-packing industry.
That judicial assistance was not tendered him was the result of his own refusal to share a trust which he had found
to be complicated, difficult, and technical.[4]

In addition to the importance of the immediate economic
benefits of the awards to the workers, which can hardly be
overestimated, an unexpected boon of a totally different
nature ensued. This was a type of fraternalization, an *en-
tente cordiale* which grew up between employers and workers.[5] In December, 1917, and during the first two weeks
of the arbitration hearings, the packers held aloof from the
workers. On no occasion did they assemble together, or even
sign the same sheet of foolscap.[6] In the two years which
followed, the representatives of the two groups came more
nearly to a common understanding. Together they waited

[1] The complete transcript of Judge Alschuler's findings and the award
appear in *The Butcher Workman*, April, 1918, pp. 1, 2, 3, 4 and in *Monthly
Review* of the United States Bureau of Labor Statistics, May, 1918, VI,
Number V, pp. 115-127.

[2] The new wage scale is printed in *The Butcher Workman*, April, 1918, p. 2.

[3] The four important awards subsequent to that of March 30, 1918, were
rendered on the following dates: February 15, 1919 (*The Butcher Workman*,
February, 1919, p. 1); December 1, 1919 (*ibid.*, December, 1919, pp. 1, 8);
April 26, 1920 (*ibid.*, January, 1921, p. 1); July 14, 1921 (*ibid.*, July, 1921,
pp. 1, 2).

[4] Mr. Daniel Cargill assisted Judge Alschuler in the work of Sioux City
and St. Paul.

[5] According to statements made by men who are its executives, employee
representation plans owe their existence to the rapprochement which was
created at this time.

[6] *Meeting of the President's Mediation Commission*, pp. 385, 387-92.

their turns to testify, hung around the old Federal Building, and lunched at neighboring restaurants. The administrator urged the elimination of professional advocates from the hearings.[1] He went even a step further. After the creation of an atmosphere of mutual respect, the contending parties not infrequently talked things over and arrived at their own decisions, which Judge Alschuler gladly 'rubberstamped.'

During 1918 and the first half of 1919, racial and nationality differences were not paramount. They were, however, utilized by the unions to elicit the sympathy of the public and of the arbitrator. Picturesqueness as well as pathos was introduced into the hearings as the arbitrator, in a kindly and painstaking manner, drew stories of poverty and degradation from foreign-born men and women. The union was careful to see that the cases involving Negro workers were adequately handled; their complaints were considered to be proportionately more numerous than those of any other group of workers. Colored people, in their rôle as packing house workers, testified at the Federal Building if concerned in the issue under discussion. An exception was the instance of Mrs. Laura Myrtle Covington, presented in court as a witness who 'represented colored girls.' Describing the conditions of employment at Wilson and Company and at the Libby, McNeill and Libby Company, she frequently alluded to the fact that 'niggers' had been secured for employment which white girls refused, and to the discrimination between the races. The court recognized that a separate complaint was being introduced, and dismissed the question of discrimination between colored and white girls on the ground that it was not included in the six questions to be arbitrated.[2]

A curious feature of the agreement which had been entered into by the packers and the workers with the President's Mediation Commission now caused a crisis: no specific

[1] The packers retained as their attorneys Mr. Carl Meyer and Mr. J. G. Condon; the Butcher Workmen were represented at the second arbitration hearing by Attorney Francis J. Heney; at the third and fourth hearings by Attorney Redmond S. Brennan.

[2] *Arbitration of Wages and Hours in the Packing-House Industry*, II, pp. 978-1022.

time limit had been set for the period of arbitration. The agreement was merely that it should remain in effect 'during the continuation of the war.' In this crisis in the relationship between the packers and unions, strength and authority passed to the packers.

In April, 1919, the five big packers requested of Secretary of Labor Wilson that the Alschuler Arbitration Agreement be extended for one year after peace had been signed with Germany, 'in order to avoid labor controversies and to promote the general welfare during the troublous period of reconstruction.' [1] The workers hesitated before entering into the second agreement,[2] but eventually signed at the request of Secretary Wilson. Direct negotiations between employers and workers, the ultimate aim of the unions, had again been postponed.[3] The ominous nature of the episode aroused the apprehension of the two contending parties; each was endeavoring to gain the favor of, and tighten its grip upon, the unskilled wage-earners.

For over a year, the leaders had concentrated their efforts upon the arbitration hearings, to the neglect of union organization. But since the goal was still a one hundred per cent organization of stockyard and packing house workers, a new campaign for membership was opened.[4] No attempt was made to present the principles and aims of a labor organization to the mass of unskilled workers; the more concrete appeal which received a ready response was the assertion

[1] See *The Butcher Workman*, March, 1921, p. 4, for texts of the notice for the renewal of the agreement sent on April 12, 1919, to Secretary of Labor Wilson by the packers, and of the letter sent to Judge Alschuler commending him for his great service and expressing a desire that he remain the administrator.

[2] *The New Majority*, May 10, 1919, pp. 1, 11.

[3] The Stock Yards Labor Council executives who opposed the signing of the second agreement claimed that it had been entered into by representatives of the A.M.C. and B.W. of N.A. without the consent or the knowledge of the workers. In addition, they asserted that the membership campaign which followed was necessitated by a diminution in union membership which registered the protest of the workers. The A.M.C. and B.W. of N.A. was charged with indifference toward the drive. The Stock Yards Labor Council accused the Butcher Workmen of forming District Council No. 9 'in opposition to the criticism surrounding the signing of the agreement.' (*The Packinghouse Worker*, October 2, 1919, pp. 1-2.) In October, 1919, the hostility between the two councils was given concrete expression in the dual publication of *The Packinghouse Worker*, the official bulletin of the trade unions in the stockyards. The Stock Yards Labor Council and District Council No. 9 each issued a publication of the same designation to present its cause to the workers.

[4] *The New Majority*, June 14, 1919, pp. 1, 6.

that the Government would give them higher wages if they
joined the organization. Within a week reports were again
favorable.[1] The encouraging response from the colored
workers[2] led the Stock Yards Labor Council to redouble
its efforts to unionize the Negroes, and to this end a 'giant
stockyards union celebration' was planned for July 6. A
workers' parade which was to include both races was scheduled to form at Forty-Seventh and Pauline Streets, to pass
through the Black Belt and halt at a public playground at
Thirty-Third and La Salle Streets, where speakers were to
address the throngs.[3] On the morning of the event, the
packers asked the police to revoke the parade permit lest a
race riot be precipitated. As the workers were not permitted to march together, two parades formed, a white and
a colored, and marched to the Beutner playgrounds where a
Negro and white audience was assembled.[4] The marchers
were greeted by cheers from the colored workers who lined
the streets, and the mounted police remained idle. One of
the placards which dotted the procession read:

The bosses think that because we are of different color and
different nationalities we should fight each other. We're going
to fool them and fight for a common cause—a square deal for
all.[5]

The demonstration was full of enthusiasm, vision, and
hope for a united group of workers. J. W. Johnstone,
secretary of the Stock Yards Labor Council, said:

It does me good to see such a checkerboard crowd—by that I
mean all of the workers here are not standing apart in groups,
one race huddled in one bunch, one nationality in another. You
are all standing shoulder to shoulder as men, regardless of
whether your face is white or black.[6]

[1] *The New Majority*, June 21, 1919, p. 13. From a column by John Riley,
colored A. F. of L. organizer, which appeared from time to time during this
period.
[2] In its day of prosperity, Local 651 started a coöperative grocery and
clothing store, the scope of which it was ambitious to extend. The enterprise
was said to be capitalized at $10,000, the shares of stock were sold at $10.
A loan of $1,000 was appropriated by the union in order to start the venture.
Ibid., August 2, 1919, p. 10.
[3] *Ibid.*, July 5, 1919, p. 15.
[4] *Ibid.*, July 12, 1919, p. 11; *ibid.*, August 9, 1919, pp. 1-2.
[5] *Ibid.*, July 12, 1919, p. 11.
[6] *Ibid.*, p. 1.

As the efforts to organize the packing house workers were redoubled, the vigilance of the police department increased. 'Cossacks' patrolled the yards; union meetings were dispersed by the intrusion of the mounted officers of the law. Finally, following a strike of protest in which approximately ten thousand workmen participated, Judge Alschuler ordered the Chief of Police to withdraw his force.[1]

Race Riots

In the same month, July, 1919, two situations culminated which put an end to the active drive for union members and marked another turning-point in the history of the unions: the Chicago race riots and the formation of District Council No. 9 by the Amalgamated Meat Cutters and Butcher Workmen of North America in direct opposition to the Stock Yards Labor Council.[2] Jealous and ambitious leaders of contending factions in the labor movement maligned one another, and union fought union under the technical guise of constitutional and jurisdictional rights; worker was brought in opposition to worker as suspicions and antagonisms were aroused by the display of racial hatred and rioting.

An account of the formation of District Council No. 9, its jurisdictional and organizational disputes with the Stock Yards Labor Council in which the Chicago and American Federations of Labor became involved, and which were manifest in the arbitration hearings before Judge Alschuler, is unnecessary for the purpose of this study. The fact cannot, however, be ignored that the internal dissensions and conflicts furthered the disruption of the packing house unions and redounded to the advantage of the employers.[3]

[1] *The New Majority*, July 26, 1919, p. 3. The stockyards police station captain was openly accused of being a 'tool of the packers.'

[2] The account of the formation of District Council No. 9 and its jurisdictional disputes with the Stock Yards Labor Council are presented in *Labor Herald*, 'Making and Breaking the Packinghouse Unions,' March, 1922, pp. 18-23; *The Butcher Workman*, August, 1919, pp. 1, 4; October, 1919, pp. 1, 2, 4; November, 1919, pp. 1, 2, 3, 5; December, 1919, pp. 1, 2; *The New Majority*, September 27, 1919, p. 10; October 25, 1919, p. 13; January 24, 1920, pp. 13-14; April 24, 1920, p. 13; May 8, 1920, p. 13; *The Packinghouse Worker*, October 2, 1919, pp. 1-2; October 18, 1919, pp. 1-3.

[3] The mechanical trades, with the exception of the steam and operating engineers, were the first to secede from the Stock Yards Labor Council and to form a council of their own. Three councils of workers were thus estab-

To what extent nationality and racial differences obstructed the feeling of unity among the packing house workers cannot be ascertained.[1]   The Amalgamated Meat Cutters and Butcher Workmen of North America and District Council No. 9 were in control of the Irish and German skilled butchers; their policies were dictated by the American Federation of Labor.   The protagonist of the unskilled Slavic workers and of the Stock Yards Labor Council was the Polish organizer, and with him were associated officials accredited with I.W.W. affiliations.   At a crucial point in yard affairs a nationality cleavage appeared, the Irish, Germans, Scandinavians, and English-speaking people turning against the south Europeans; the more skilled workmen rebelled against the dictatorship of the foreign-born rank and file and against admitting them upon a basis of equality within the ranks of the Butcher Workmen.[2]   The language barrier again became an almost insurmountable handicap— the isolation of the foreign workers was utilized to increase their dependence upon their own leaders.   The 'peasants' were threatened by members of their own nationality that failure to uphold the Stock Yards Labor Council would result in a return to former conditions of employment, and

lished among the trade-unions and employees in the slaughtering and meatpacking industry. *The Butcher Workman*, November, 1919, p. 2. See William Z. Foster, *Misleaders of Labor* (Chicago: The Trade Union Educational League, 1927), pp. 159-61.

[1] From 1906 to 1920, the *Convention Proceedings* of the A.M.C. and B.W. of N.A. refer to the changing nationalities of the workers, or which the following examples are typical: In 1906, a resolution was passed authorizing the publication of part of the *Official Journal* in the German language, and the appointment of a German organizer. It also went on record 'as opposed to the filling of this country with a cheap class of labor that does not intend to establish homes and become honorable citizens of this commonwealth.' (*Report of Proceedings*, 1906, pp. 45, 68.) In 1917, a resolution was presented asking for the publication of organizers' reports in the Polish and Lithuanian languages. The request was referred to the executive committee and was granted. (*Ibid.*, 1917, pp. 114-15, 139.) At the Tenth General Convention a '100 per cent American' resolution was passed to the effect that all officers, international or local, and all organizers should be citizens of the country in which they were residing, or become such as soon as the laws could be complied with. *Ibid.*, 1920, p. 130.

[2] Each local union, regardless of its size, was given representation to the extent of five delegates in District Council No. 9. The laws governing the District Council were drafted by the Executive Board under instructions of the General Convention of the A.M.C. and B.W. of N.A. in 1917. The laws were never approved by any convention. The Tenth General Convention in 1920 passed a resolution giving to each District Council the right to decide the question of its own representation and taxation. *Report of Proceedings*, 1920, pp. 180-81.

that since they could not speak the English language, they would be clubbed into submission by sluggers and soon fill the jails.[1]

In the official and journalistic literature on the subject, the dates of the Chicago race riot are given as July 27 to August 2, 1919.[2] No group in the entire community was more affected than the stockyard workers; no issue was more irrevocably determined as a result of it than the labor policy which was to prevail in the packing houses.

Racial differences and antagonism were present in the problems of housing, education, social relationships, economic equality, and legal status; but by July 27, 1919, the conflict between the packing house employers and workers for the allegiance of the Negroes had become so sharp that each laid the responsibility for the race riot upon the other. At its conclusion an almost impregnable barrier had been erected, which brought to an abrupt end the Negroes' trade-union experience.[3]

[1] *Glose Rabotnica*, August 31, 1919 (*Labor's Voice*, Polish paper owned and published by John Kikulski).

[2] All records of the race riot include the stockyards district among the geographical divisions in which the disorders took place. The two sections in which the worst clashes occurred were the Black Belt, and the district on the South Side, including the yards and 'Packingtown,' bounded by the Chicago River on the north, and Fifty-Fifth Street on the south, and on the east by Wentworth Avenue. Thirty-four per cent of the injured received their wounds in the Black Belt, 41 per cent in the district including the stockyards. (*The Negro in Chicago*, p. 9.) This particular district was the home of white gangs or 'athletic clubs'; the 'Canaryville bunch' and the 'Hamburg bunch,' and the famous 'Ragen's Colts,' all of which were accredited with political affiliation of more or less importance. According to a report of the state's attorney of Cook County: . . . more bank robbers, pay-roll bandits, automobile bandits, highwaymen, and strong-arm crooks come from this particular district than from any other that has come to his notice during seven years of service as chief prosecuting official.' *Ibid.*, p. 8, as quoted in Carl Sandburg, *The Chicago Race Riots*, chap. I, p. 1., New York: Harcourt, Brace and Howe, 1919.)

Wentworth Avenue was designated as the 'dead line' by the police. West of it no Negroes were allowed to go; east of it, no white men and women. In order to reach their work in the yards, the Negroes who lived east of Wentworth Avenue had to traverse the area in which the white "hoodlums' were creating the worst disorders in Chicago. The risk involved kept many of them from work. The packing companies immediately made arrangements for their workers to receive unpaid wages at the Chicago Urban League, the Young Men's Christian Association, the South Side Community Service House, and the Binga State Bank; they opened relief stations and supplemented the work of the Red Cross in dispensing food. *The Negro in Chicago*, p. 44.

[3] The increase of the Negro population in Chicago from 1910 to 1920 was from 44,103 to 109,594, or 148.5 per cent. The increase in white population, including foreign immigrants, was 21 per cent. The years of heaviest Negro migration were 1916-18, when half a million Negroes moved from the

As the race riot began on Sunday afternoon, most workers had knowledge of it before leaving their residences on
Monday morning. Thus many disturbances may have been
averted. A small percentage of packing house employees
reported for work; during the day members of both races
peacefully handled the usual tools of their trade. In the
afternoon, as Negroes returned to their homes, malicious
attacks were made upon them.[1] White and Negro men who
attempted to reach the yards on Tuesday morning were assaulted. From then until Saturday, minor cases of violence
were reported throughout the district, but there was no
acute cause for alarm. On Saturday morning at three-
thirty, one of the most serious events of the entire period of
rioting occurred. Nine hundred and forty-eight people living
west of the yards were made homeless by fires. The press
was quick to interpret their incendiary origin as retaliatory
and to suspect the Negroes. All the houses burned were
owned by Lithuanians. Investigation failed to fix the guilt
upon Negroes as a group, or upon individual colored men.[2]
The superintendent of Swift and Company said that he
'understood there was as much friction between the Poles
and Lithuanians . . . as between the Negroes and the
whites.' The grand jury reported: 'The jury believes that
these fires were started for the purpose of inciting race
feeling by blaming same on the blacks.'[3] The superintendent of Armour and Company, when questioned, testified as
follows:

southern to the northern states. It was estimated that within a period of
eighteen months in 1917-18 more than 50,000 Negroes came to Chicago. *The
Negro in Chicago*, p. 79.

[1] Henry Goodman, a Negro, was knocked down and beaten. He died as
a result of wounds. Nicholas Kleinmark, a white man, was a member of a
mob which attacked Negroes who were returning from work in the yards.
He died of a stab wound. (*The Negro in Chicago*, pp. 656, 659.) ' . . . the
members of a white "gang" . . . were stationed at a gateway into the
yards, each man with a club, and each beating a colored man on his way
home from work at the close of the day. On one occasion, within a block of
the Settlement, Settlement residents prevented a group of one race driving
a team of horses and heavy laden wagon over the prostrate body of a member
of the other race, who had been knocked unconscious. . . .' *Mary McDowell
Neighbor*, p. 175.

[2] The Negroes in the city were appreciative of the thorough manner in
which the origins of the fires were investigated. The foreign-born were advised of their innocence. Every priest and clergyman in the fire-stricken
district aided in the movement, which had the support of the Chancellor of the
Catholic archdiocese of Chicago. *The Chicago Defender*, August 9, 1919.

[3] *The Negro in Chicago*, pp. 20-21, 539-40.

. . . I believe it goes without saying that there isn't a colored man, regardless of how little brains he'd have, who would attempt to go over into the Polish district and set fire to anybody's house over there. He wouldn't get that far.[1]

Bitterness and friction accompanied the attempt of the colored workmen to return to their positions in the yards. The packers asked the members of Local 651 to postpone return until adequate protection could be provided for them. On Monday, August 5, two days after the fire, the union members were notified that arrangement had been made with the militia for bayonet and machine-gun defense.[2] Because of the protests of the Stock Yards Labor Council, whose contact with the Polish and Lithuanian workers made them fear a resumption of the riot, the arrival of the militia was postponed for several days.

Meanwhile, a plan whereby colored and white workers could amicably return to work was formulated by the aggressive colored trade-unionist, Mr. I. H. Bratton, and endorsed by the Stock Yards Labor Council and the Chicago Federation of Labor. The unions asked that instead of summoning troops, the employers should establish the closed-shop plan. The unions claimed that they could thereby assume responsibility for the personal conduct of all workers in the yards. After a night of dramatic but vain attempts to communicate with, and to present this plan to those who occupied positions of authority in the state and city, the members of Local 651, awaiting news at union headquarters, were rejoined in the gray of early morning by their defeated leader.

The organized laborers refused to be coerced into working under the rifles, bayonets, and machine guns of soldiers, police, and deputies, and thousands of them struck.[3] The militia also protested against this service and after a few

---

[1] *The Negro in Chicago*, pp. 20-21.

[2] *The New Majority*, August 9, 1919, pp. 2, 14. The plan was devised by the superintendent of one of the packing companies together with Adjutant-General Dickson of the militia and First Deputy Superintendent of Police Alcock. The representatives of organized labor were excluded from the meeting. Judge Alschuler was not consulted.

[3] This strike was authorized by the Stock Yards Labor Council and not by the A.M.C. and B.W. of N.A. and District Council No. 9. *The Butcher Workman*, August, 1919, p. 1.

days were withdrawn.[1] The workers were ordered to return to the yards. About six hundred white and colored laborers delayed a day and were dismissed. When the matter of the dismissal was referred to Judge Alschuler, he upheld it because of violation of the non-strike clause in the agreement.[2] The workers thus lost their seniority and pension rights, although many secured packing house work. Again racial differences and hatreds had been aroused and the breach widened between the packers and organized labor.

The Stock Yards Labor Council and the Chicago Federation of Labor worked incessantly in the city and in the yards throughout the two weeks of active disorder to steady their members.[3] The following editorial, published at the inception of the riot, clearly indicates not only the members' sympathy in the crisis through which the Negroes as a group were passing, but also appreciation of the danger to the strength and existence of the union.

Let any white union worker who has ever been on strike where gunmen or machine guns have been brought in and turned on him and his fellows search his memory and recall how he felt. In this critical moment let every union man remember the tactics of the boss in a strike, when he tries by shooting to terrorize striking workers into violence to protect themselves. Well, that is how the negroes feel. They are panic-stricken over the prospect of being killed.

. . . .

Right now it is going to be decided whether the colored workers are to continue to come into the labor movement or whether they are to feel that they have been abandoned by it and lose confidence in it.

. . . .

[1] *The New Majority*, August 16, 1919, pp. 1-2, and *The Packinghouse Worker*, 'The Chicago Race Riots,' October 18, 1919, p. 2.
[2] *The New Majority*, August 23, 1919, p. 14. Judge Alschuler, in recounting the incident, noted the fact that the case came before him as one on reinstatement following a voluntary cessation of work. The racial issue was not made use of in court despite the fact that all parties were aware that they were dealing with a 'race strike.'
[3] At the time of the riot, the colored strike-breakers at the Corn Products Refining Company at Argo had been armed with rifles and revolvers. (*Ibid.,* August 2, 1919, p. 4.) During the succeeding months, racial antagonisms were present in the controversies in the steel industry and at the McCormick Company in Chicago.

All the influence of the unions should be exerted on the community to protect colored fellow workers from the unreasoning frenzy of race prejudice. Indications of the past have been that organized labor has gone farther in eliminating race hatred than any other class. It is up against the acid test now to show whether this is so.[1]

As a result of the quality of leadership demonstrated by the union officials, the white and colored union men sustained each other in the main and ministered to the stricken. The financial aid and moral support which the union colored men received during the riot and immediately following it served to bring them to the headquarters of their organization and to keep them 'out of the packers' bread line.' [2]

But obstacles to their reëmployment were raised; the packers had hired non-union colored men because of the refusal and fear of the union members to work, first, without protection during the riot, and second, with that of the militia at the beginning of the week of readjustment. The slack period in the industry prolonged the unemployment of the Negroes who remained staunch union members. As economic necessity forced them to secure work, however, the industry and the union were abandoned.

That no violence occurred within the establishments after the return of the workers has continued to be spoken of as a noteworthy feature of the disturbances in view of the men's access to, and skill in the use of knives and cleavers. A representative of one of the largest packing companies, when questioned on this point during the investigation of the Chicago Commission on Race Relations, said:

. . . the morning that the Negroes were brought back to work in this packing house there was not a single argument—there wasn't a single indication in this plant of any racial feeling. In fact, the two classes of common labor we have are the Slavs and the Negroes and they met as old friends. In many instances they put their arms around one another's necks. In one particular instance a Negro and a Pole got on an elevated truck

[1] *The New Majority*, August 2, 1919, p. 1.
[2] See *Ibid.*, August 9, 1919, p. 8, for copies of the resolutions passed by Local 651 and other colored trade-unionists immediately following the race riots.

and rode all around this plant simply to signify to the rest of
the workers that there was a good spirit existing between the
two. There was nothing in the contact between the Negro and
the Pole or the Slav that would indicate that there had ever
been a race riot in Chicago, and there was nothing from the
beginning of the race riot to the end that would indicate that
there was any feeling started in the Stock Yards or in this
industry that led up to the race riot.[1]

The foreman of a second meat-packing establishment re-
counted the following incident:

On the day that the race riot broke, I was a member of the white
ball team which was playing our Negro team in the middle of
the Black Belt. When the rioting started our Negro men were
very greatly concerned for our safety. We finished the game
and at its conclusion the colored men insisted upon accompanying us to the elevated train, a precaution which we thought
unnecessary. After the period of rioting was over, the Negroes
and whites continued to work together as formerly. You would
never have known from conditions within the plant, that there
had been a riot in the city. The matter died down immediately
at work.

Of the thirty-eight deaths recorded during the riot, those
of one Negro, Henry Goodman, and two white men, Nicholas Kleinmark and Joseph Powers, were due to conflicts
which occurred as wage-earners were going to or returning
from their employment in the packing houses.[2] Only in the
case of William Dozier did the violence occur in the yards.[3]
The coroner's jury reported on the case as follows:

Dozier, Negro, approached a meat curer employed in the superintendent's office of Swift & Co. to ask if the Negroes were not
going to have protection in the Yards that morning. A white
worker stepped out of the crowd and struck at Dozier with a
hammer. Dozier dodged and caught the blow on the neck. He
started to run east on Exchange Avenue. As he ran he was

[1] *The Negro in Chicago*, pp. 399-400.
[2] The most horrible rumors of the entire period centered about foul Bubbly
Creek which for so many years served as a dumping ground for the decomposed
substances from the packing companies. *Ibid.*, pp. 32-33, 579-71.
[3] *Ibid.*, pp. 655-67.

struck with a street broom and shovel and other missiles; near
the sheep pens a brick felled him.   The meat curer above mentioned and an assistant identified one Zarka as the man who
wielded the hammer.   Joseph Scezak was identified as the man
who used the broom.   The coroner's jury recommended that
these two be held to the grand jury on a charge of manslaughter
and also that the unknown participants be held upon the same
charge.   Zarka and Scezak were indicted for murder, and on
May 6, 1920, a verdict of not guilty was returned as to each.[1]

Thus the '100 per cent or bust' campaign for unionization had come to an abrupt end.   Nevertheless, the officials
of the Amalgamated Meat Cutters and Butcher Workmen
of North America and the Negro organizers made a final
gesture and effort to reach the colored workmen.[2]   To this
end the colored organizers proposed a new plan, of which
the chief element was the slow but constructive work of
acquainting colored men and women with the nature of
the packing house situation, and more specifically with the
organization of labor which needed their support.   At the
conclusion of a race riot, men could no longer be aroused
by bombastic and oratorical attempts to portray the improve-
ments in conditions to be realized by a united group of
workmen, nor could the services of the Government be en-
larged upon to advantage.   Even the threat of a return to
pre-war conditions was unavailing when dealing with the
Negroes who had so recently joined the industry.

The colored organizers busied themselves in futile routine.
Their membership returns were negligible, notwithstanding
the reduction of the local's initiation fee to $3.50 which in-
cluded the dues for the first month.[3]   Their chief activity
lay in constituting themselves a grievance committee, receiving the complaints of the colored workmen and presenting
them to the District Council for redress.   Their fondest

---

[1] *The Negro in Chicago*, p. 667.
[2] At the Tenth General Convention of the A.M.C. and B.W. of N.A. 1920,
the need of organizing colored workers and of eliminating race prejudice in
the South was recognized.   A resolution was submitted which provided for
the representation of colored workers on the Executive Board, said executive
officer or officers to have general districts.   *Report of Proceedings*, pp. 6, 113.
[3] The usual initiation fee was $3, the monthly dues, $1.50.   The Negroes
claim that this amount was rarely collected from them, as the union gave
them liberal 'spensations.'

hope of utilizing the Negro press to present the claims of
trade-unionism was unrealized.[1]   They found themselves
unable to visit and to speak before local unions.   The colored ministerial association welcomed them less cordially
than before; clergymen, who had witnessed the cancellation
of the church debt in a few months during the period of
employment and the prosperity born of the War, were opposed to any organization which might bring fewer opportunities for work in the yards.

The Introduction of Employee Representation

On February 21, 1921, a few days previous to the exit of
the Wilson administration, and before the date set for the
termination of the second agreement between the unions
and packers, the packers attempted to violate it, declaring
that the exigencies in the industrial world which had justi-
fied its making were at an end.   And to prove their claim
of freedom from the administration, they announced a wage
reduction to take effect March 14, 1921,[2] and the expediency
of a return to the ten-hour workday.   The unions now
openly accused the employers of trying to take advantage of
them at the moment when conditions became unfavorable,[3]

[1] On August 23, 1919, *The Chicago Defender* published an article entitled
'Shall We Unionize?'   The leaders of the Stock Yards Labor Council had
solicited without success the aid of the leading colored newspaper as a means
of telling the workingmen of trade-unionism, and of dispensing information
during the race riots.   In the article referred to, the editor mentions a conference with Kikulski, Fitzpatrick, and Johnstone at which these leaders
asserted that the black workman would be protected by his white associates in
the ranks of organized labor.   The Negro editor concludes that it may be the
part of wisdom to join the trade-unions.   *The Butcher Workman,* January,
1921, pp. 1, 2, carried an article signed by Mr. Bratton in which the colored
oranizer makes a plea to all workers to join the union movement.
[2] At a convention called in Omaha, March 9 and 10, the A.M.C. and B.W. of
N.A. surveyed the situation and drew up resolutions of protest which were com-
municated to President Harding.   The Executive Committee of the union was
authorized to represent them in a conference called by Secretary of Labor Davis
on March 21, 1921.   'Conference table rather than settlement table after conflict and suffering' was the policy adopted.   The convention authorized a strike
ballot which was sent to workers in the packing industry in the United States
and Canada.   The ballot read as follows: 'Do you favor and authorize a strike
in the event that the government of our organization is unable to induce the
packers to maintain the eight-hour workday in compliance with the agreement
entered into by the United States Department of Labor?'   *Ibid.,* March, 1921,
pp. 1-2.
[3] A comparative statement of cash receipts and disbursements from August
1, 1919, to June 30, 1920, shows that the disbursement for organizing was
$277,901, an increase of $158,920 over that of the previous twelve months,

and at their behest Secretaries Davis, Hoover, and Wallace of the new Harding administration prevailed upon the packers to sign a third agreement for a period of six months, which was to expire on September 15, 1921.[1] By acceptance of a wage-cut,[2] the union received the support of the Government in maintaining the basic eight-hour day, overtime rates, seniority rights, and other provisions established during the arbitration proceedings.

While the union officials had been occupied with the arbitration proceedings, the personnel in the packing companies had undergone a tremendous change because of the World War, the restriction of immigration, and the more trying reconstruction period. The stirring organization campaign for union members in 1918, with its record of fourteen hundred converts who 'came forward' at one meeting, was forgotten. Internal dissension and factionalism, a 'boring from within,' had sapped the energy of the Butcher Workmen; the Chicago race riots had supplied a second disrupting factor. Not only was organized labor weakened; its position was disadvantageous. The individuals constituting the rank and file of the industry no longer concerned themselves with conditions in the packing houses; the fear, the terror of unemployment was gripping men and women.

The six months of truce and continued arbitration became a period of mobilization.[3] Judge Alschuler urged upon packers and workers the formation and adoption of a concrete

which had shown an increase in expenditure for this one item of $61,368 over the period of August 1, 1917, to July 31, 1918. From August 1, 1919, to June 30, 1920, the total disbursements of the union exceeded the receipts by $71,165. At the beginning of the year June 30, 1920, the union had on hand $4,113; it closed the year with $935, not including Liberty Bonds to the amount of $5,100. *Report of Proceedings, 1920*, p. 210; *Report of Proceedings of the Eleventh General Convention*, A.M.C. and B.W. of N.A., 1922, p. 34.

[1] *The Butcher Workman*, April, 1921, p. 1.

[2] The acceptance of the wage reduction, which occurred without the authority of the Federal Administrator, marks the beginning of direct negotiation between the packers and workers.

[3] In July, 1921, a wage reduction, requested by the packers, was refused by Judge Alschuler. Statements of the packers and the workers are contained in 'Application for change in wage rates and working conditions in packing houses operating under an agreement with the President's Mediation Commission and Secretary of Labor; and David J. Saposs and Olive Rabe, The Labor Bureau, Inc. 'Answer of the Amalgamated Meat Cutters and Butcher Workmen of North America to the Application of Employers for a Reduction in Wage Rates in the Packing Houses Operating under Arbitration Agreements.'

plan whereby the relationship which had been of common benefit could be perpetuated; he pointed out the advisability of anticipating the time when they would have to deal directly with each other. When the Secretary of Labor became cognizant of the fact that the packers were contemplating the installation of employee representation plans,[1] he asked them to sign the six months' extension of the agreement. Now they hastened to perfect their plans and put them into operation before the summer had passed.[2] The unions, and more especially the Amalgamated Meat Cutters and Butcher Workmen of North America, mapped out their line of action: the strengthening of their ranks by an increase in membership, the creation of a dollar a week emergency fund in every local, and the preparation of the demands which they hoped would be incorporated in an agreement with the packers.

Seemingly possessed with an insatiable enthusiasm for drives, the unions set out to duplicate former plans and concentrate upon organizing the stockyard workers. Officers and organizers voluntarily cut their salaries to secure the funds necessary for the campaign. Addressing a mass meeting of fifteen thousand workers on June 19, President Cornelius J. Hayes of the Amalgamated Meat Cutters and Butcher Workmen of North America congratulated the Slavic laborers because in most places they now formed the backbone of the packing house union. He dubbed as slackers the men and women of American birth who were the doers of odd jobs, aspiring to escape from manual work, and Negroes. He gave an historical sketch to explain the succession of national and racial groups in the yards.

We too have a colored problem but I am going to say that in most packing centers the negro is beginning to see the light.

[1] Clemen, *op. cit.*, p. 722, and Swift and Company, 'Memorandum of the Strike Situation in the Packing Industry.'

[2] On June 21, 1921, the A.M.C. and B.W. of N.A. charged the packers with gross violation of at least six of the fundamental provisions of the Alschuler Administration, namely, Provisions No. 1, No. 2, No. 3, No. 7, No. 10, No. 12. The creation of the company unions was alleged to interfere with the right of an employee to choose his or her representative to present grievances. In order to initiate and set the Industrial Relations Plans in motion, employees were said to have been compelled by threat and intimidation to choose representatives. Further trade-union activity was met with acts of discrimination. *The Butcher Workman*, July, 1921, pp. 1, 2.

He is beginning to see that he must stand up for right and jus-
tice. For only that method can advance. You know there is
some excuse for the poor, illiterate negro, coming from the
plantations and cotton fields, drawn to the North by stories
of undreamed wealth, unused to any semblance of fair wages,
suffering being his usual lot. No wonder the poor black man
hesitates and knows not where to turn. Then unfortunately
there are some of his own race, those who ought to lead him,
posing as Christians, who give him bad advice, who preach to
him to keep away from the Union, impressing him 'it biteth
like a snake and stingeth like an adder,' and they forget that
those bad things were said about the Union Carpenter of Naz-
areth, and he, like our Union, wanted to help the world. For-
tunately many of our good colored brothers understand and
they are preaching the gospel of unity and they declaim both
loud and long that wage slavery is not one whit better than
chattel slavery and the black man, the negro, must come into
the union, which knows neither creed, color, or nationality, the
A.M.C. and B.W. of N.A.

The packer, or rather his representatives are full of varied
devices to beat down the union. Nationality is played against
nationality, color against color—even religious questions are
brought in as though it were any difference whether you be
Mohammedan or Christian, Jew or Gentile, Atheist or otherwise
in this game of life. . . .[1]

I see before me now men of various nationalities—Poles,
Lithuanians, Russians, Negroes, and fifty-seven other kinds.
Was it always this way in the packing industry? Not so. I can
remember when the son of the Emerald Isle, the Irishman, the
offshoot of Carl Schurz, the German, and a few Yankees were
the bulk of the help. Well, you say, what caused them to leave?
Why, the packer. Those men, good butchers, good packing-
house men, began to balk in harness, began to think organization. Then the packer thought he would enlist the aid of the
Bohemian, Pole, Slav, etc. And so they came to the plant,
those hardy sons of Southern Europe, fleeing from persecution.
The packer, in his junker style, thought he would make tools
of them, but to the glory of those Slavish people, they saw,
they understood and today the Pole, the Bohemian, the Lithuanian, the Slav, the Croatian, etc., are among our best, very
best, citizens, and that means union men.

[1] *The Butcher Workman*, June, 1921, p. 3.

A few years ago the packers conceived the idea of using the black man to beat down his fellow men of other complexion. So they sent their emissaries down to the cotton fields of the Sunny South—the Mississippi plantation. They sang to them songs of the glorious North. They told them of high wages and short workdays. They painted to them the glorious pictures of heaven on earth. And thus the colored men came to the packing centers in droves. Many of them were men of vision and they saw, they understood and they became members of our union. Some of them are our best workers and the rest of them are thinking, thinking every day. I know eventually the colored man, who has made wonderful progress despite adversity, will eventually be one hundred per cent union.

The packer, too, sees this, and I know, my friends, that Wendell Phillips, Lovejoy, Garrison, the immortal Lincoln, the foremost champion of the negro, would be ashamed to know that some are not standing up to be counted, are afraid. Can you imagine Abraham Lincoln a scab, Wendell Phillips a strike-breaker, Lovejoy an informer, Garrison a non-believer? No, you cannot. The spirit of Lincoln, Lovejoy, Wendell Phillips, *et al.* beckons to you, colored people, from the throne above the skies and bids you to be faithful to your trust and proud of your heritage and to join the Butchers' Union. The packer, too, feels this. In many places he is introducing a new element, a new race of people, the Mexican, to work in the packing industry. He won't have to wait very long ere the poor peon shall learn, as many successful strikes in his own country proclaim.[1]

Extensive publicity was given to the venture to organize the colored man. The aid of Negro political and social leaders was solicited; the ministry was again appealed to in an effort to reach the colored worker through the persons to whom he was most accustomed to look for guidance.[2] The colored organizers again attempted to strengthen Local 651.[3] The greatest response was shown at a mass meeting at Unity Hall which six hundred colored workers attended. In

[1] *The Butcher Workman,* July, 1921, p. 7.
[2] *The New Majority,* December 17, 1921, p. 6. L. B. Anderson, alderman of the second ward, promised his support. On December 12, the Baptist Alliance conferred with the Council for the purpose of organizing the colored workers. (*Ibid.,* December 24, 1921, p. 6.) Reverend Watson, chairman of the Joint Church Movement of the State of Illinois, was interviewed.
[3] *The Butcher Workman,* November, 1921, p. 12.

addition to the Butcher Workmen, representatives from the Pullman porters, the car cleaners, hotel and restaurant workers, and musicians were present. A movement to start a central council of Negro unions was initiated. Following the stirring remarks of John Fitzpatrick, Oscar DePriest, and Mrs. Irene Goins, an organizing committee was formed.[1] But the results obtained by the committee and paid organizers were very small. From hectic impotent activity Local 651 entered a state of quiescence from which it was never aroused.

A month before the expiration of the Alschuler agreement the Amalgamated Meat Cutters and Butcher Workmen of North America, at a meeting at Omaha, August 15, 16, and 17, formulated their demands for a continuation of the wage-scale and working conditions then in effect, changes to occur only by common agreement or by arbitration. When approached by Amalgamated Meat Cutters and Butcher Workmen of North America representatives on September 7,[2] the packers refused to negotiate the agreement. The rebuff had been anticipated, and the union now asked for a strike vote in the various packing centers hoping to force thereby recognition from the packers.[3] The workers were unmoved by the warnings of their union leaders concerning 'so-called' employee representation plans,[4] but the first

[1] *The New Majority*, December 3, 1921, p. 2. The members of the Steering Committee were: N. S. Wims, president of the Pullman Porters; I. H. Bratton, secretary of the Butcher Workmen; Henry Sherfie, treasurer of the Butcher Workmen; G. Strauther, J. P. Brown, G. W. Downing, of the Butcher Workmen; P. D. Campbell, of the Hotel and Restaurant Employees; E. M. Scott, of the Pullman Porters; A. Wilcher and Dr. W. D. Cook, D.D.

[2] *The Butcher Workman*, September, 1921, pp. 1, 2.

[3] The union announced that 85 per cent of its members had voted in favor of a strike. *Ibid.*, October, 1921, p. 1.

[4] In December, 1917, Wilson and Company established a 'Progress Committee' which was the forerunner of plans of employee representation. Its 'Joint Representative Committee' was introduced in March, 1921. (Wilson and Company *Year Book*, 1921.) On March 15, 1921, at Armour and Company, employee representatives were elected to meet with management representatives. Swift and Company had been experimenting with plans in three of its small plants and on May 16, 1921, inaugurated an 'Employees' Representation Plan' in the Chicago plant. (Swift and Company *Year Book*, 1922.) Copies of the plans of employee representation used by the packing companies are published and readily available. (See the pamphlet *Employees' Representation in Industry*, issued by the Institute of American Meat Packers, March, 1927.) After 1907, subsequent to the organization of Employee Benefit Associations by Swift and Company, the larger packers put into operation the following departments looking to the welfare of their workmen: Employment, Medical, Casualty, Employee Relations, Pension, and Employee's Stock Savings; health

act of the assemblies in lowering wages shook them from their complacency. On November 17, the question of wage reduction was referred to the plant assemblies. Seventy-five per cent of the members voted in favor of it. Following the announcement that it would become effective November 28, the Amalgamated Meat Cutters and Butcher Workmen of North America called a strike for Monday, December 5.

Although each side tried to establish its will under the guise of democracy, the packers were the stronger. The Butcher Workmen overreached themselves in claiming jurisdiction over the affairs of laborers in the entire industry. The unionization of the stockyards was not sufficient to justify such a claim if made on behalf of all the yard unions; still less when put forward by the butchers' union alone. On the other hand, the packers forced upon the workers the plans of employee representation which they themselves formulated, justifying the procedure by pointing to the high percentage of workmen which had voted for the adoption of the plans. At the two elections held during the month, representatives of the workers who were not in a position to cast ballots intelligently decided issues of far-reaching importance, acting as the tools of those who occupied positions of authority.

The daily press echoed in its news section the packers' evaluation of the 1921 strike.[1] Only brief reports of an occasional riot, of a petition for, and the granting of a temporary injunction by Judge Denis E. Sullivan,[2] of the efforts of state and federal officials, to bring peace,[3] of the activities of the one hundred policemen in the yards, and of 'work, as usual,'[4] crept into the newspapers.

The livestock market reports revealed a situation not wholly favorable to the packing companies.[5] The strike

and recreational features were introduced; educational activities were promoted which took the form of continuation schools, plant publications, English and Americanization classes, and, lastly, training classes for foremen and the office force.

[1] *The Butcher Workman,* December, 1921, p. 12, contains a summary of accounts of the strike which appeared in the daily press.
[2] *The Chicago Daily News,* December 8, 1921, p. 1.
[3] *Ibid.,* December 9, 1921, p. 1; December 10, 1921, p. 3.
[4] *Ibid.,* December 20, 1921, p. 3.
[5] *Ibid.,* December 12 to December 23, 1921, inclusive.

was forcing a curtailment of operations.   Shippers were advised not to send cattle into Chicago.   A warning went forth to 'hold all livestock in the feed lots.' [1]

The weeks immediately preceding and following the holiday season were grim for those who walked the streets in the vicinity of 'Packingtown.'   The wage-cut struck the key for the festival season.   Workers became destitute.[2]   Normal production could not be resumed.[3]   The employers continued to face a grave state of affairs at a time of year when output was usually at its height.   But more than this, they were again participants in a conflict with an adversary of prodigious vitality and determination.   The packers had met the tenacity of the Amalgamated Meat Cutters and Butcher Workmen of North America with similar tenacity. In the effort 'to bring about better understanding and co-operation in industry,' the employee representation plans had been created.   The packers conceded that they alone must assume, not only the initiative in forming the plans, but also the responsibility for the results.[4]   But before the schemes could be 'sold' to the workers and the elected assembly representatives properly introduced to their new duties and opportunities, it was imperative to eliminate the necessity for an agreement with the Butcher Workmen. The disparity in the relative strength of the packers and of the unions presaged a conclusive conflict of short duration.

The methods used by the packers and the unions in December, 1921, and in January, 1922, were merely a repetition and an intensification of the adroit devices employed during previous strikes, particularly in the use of the Negro. But in the seventeen years between 1904 and 1921, conditions had changed so that the Negro was faced with a choice

[1] *Chicago Daily Drovers' Journal,* December 19, 1921, as quoted in *The New Majority,* December 31, 1921, p. 3.
[2] 'Christmas at the Yards,' *The New Majority,* December 24, 1921, p. 4.
[3] *The Chicago Daily News,* December 28, 1921, p. 28, as quoted in *The Butcher Workman,* January, 1922, p. 1.   *Chicago Daily Drovers' Journal,* December 28, December 30, 1921, and January 6, 1922, as quoted in *The Butcher Workman,* January, 1922, p. 1.   *The Chicago Daily Tribune,* January 9, 1922, as quoted in *The Butcher Workman,* January, 1922, p. 1.
[4] Institute of American Meat Packers, 'Employees' Representation in Industry,' p. 11.

of giving allegiance to the packers' or the workers' organizations. In the face of an emergncy which involved a decision as unequivocal as this, the Negro faltered only momentarily.[1] To him the choice was between a job and no job; economic necessity was so great that primary needs determined his fealty. He sought favor and protection where they were to be found; lip service to the union was abandoned.

The southern colored workingman in the northern city possessed few qualifications and little training or skill to commend him for a position in the slaughtering or meat-packing divisions of a highly mechanized industry. But he preceded the northern Negro into the establishments. By training and experience he was generally an agriculturist from the decaying tobacco, cotton, and cane fields. The former domestic continued to make personal bargains for wages, and to look up to a boss who would both understand his irregularities as a worker and sympathize with his more personal interests. In his economic world the boss had always been the possessor of power. As long as he had remained humble he had been taken care of. On the southern plantation his alignment with wealth and power was traditional; the size of the master's holdings was an opportunity for an expression of his pride. His emotional response to northern industry was similar. He looked upon his employer as his patron and provider and in the Chicago stockyards the employer was 'kind' to him. Whatever racial prejudice individuals who composed the management group may have had, it was not kindled into active opposition either by a threatened impingement upon personal status or by imminent economic competition. Work could not be furnished him by members of his own race. In 1918 and 1919, the increase in Negro employment on the killing floor and in the preparation of by-products in the great abattoirs was an unparalleled boon.

Few Negro laborers possessed a conviction of the fundamental economic advantages of collective bargaining and of

---

[1] At the beginning of hostilities the statement was published that Local 651 was 100 per cent strong in the strike. (*The Butcher Workman*, December, 1921, p. 3.) The local, however, was too weak to function.

the united advance which labor must make if its attainments were to be effective and permanent. That the gains of all workingmen were of prime consequence to a race composed principally of manual laborers, or that the unions would be unavailing without them, were truths only dimly discerned. In the absence of industrial class consciousness, the query at the decisive moment was, 'What has the Butchers' Union ever done for us, and what has it to offer us now?'

Southern Negroes were vaguely aware that trade-unions had not admitted them whole-heartedly or on the basis of equality. First-hand experience was limited, but Booker T. Washington had voiced the accusation; this was sufficient evidence for them. Northern colored workingmen who had succeeded in entering industries had gained their positions without the help of, often in spite of unions, as scabs when the white men went out on strike. Again, if one achieved the rôle of skilled worker, it was not infrequently in the face of opposition by organized labor, which was endeavoring to prohibit Negro apprentices in many trades. In 1903, the Negro waiters in Chicago who participated in the Kohlsaat strike broadcast their conviction that organized labor had 'double-crossed' them. This experience and propaganda they now revived to discredit the motives of the Butcher Workmen. In the yards, the colored man had sensed the fact that as a colored trade-unionist his position was anomalous and precarious: if forced to recognize and to employ members of labor organizations, the employers would quickly dispense with as great a number of colored unionists as the available labor supply would permit.

To be sure, there was another side to employment in the yards and to the position of the unions which might have led the colored man to a sympathetic support of organized labor. The Negro had undertaken the most undesirable tasks—employment in the hide-cellars, the 'gut-shanties,' and the 'bone-house,' and in the making of fertilizer. For a time this had been satisfactory. Had not every race and nationality group in the yards accepted work on identical terms and risen by the same process? But whereas in a

short time other workmen received recognition for acceptable work through promotions and permanent employment,
the majority of the Negroes remained common and seasonal
laborers. And following the labor controversies, when he
filled the void left by strikers, the Negro not infrequently
found himself an outcast despite the employment which
had been accepted, and which involved considerable personal
risk and danger. Yes, the employer was discriminating
against him, treating him as a member of a distinct group
whose surplus of inexperienced but cheap and docile labor
could be utilized in an emergency.

The Chicago Federation of Labor and the Stock Yards
Labor Council endeavored to give the workers an understanding of the position in which colored people were placed
during the race riots. In spite of this, and the absence of
discriminatory acts during the arbitration proceedings, the
conflicts which occurred in 1919 in the district and the
propaganda instituted by the packers and the Negro leaders
aggravated the lurking distrust from which the Negro had
not freed himself. He feared the hostility and opposition
with which members of the white race would meet his attempt at economic security. He became convinced that the
equality implied by the juxtaposition of members of the two
races within the workshop could not be sustained; that the
contacts and competition on an economic plane which the
union provided would tend to sharpen rather than to eliminate race prejudice. Inevitably the white man would see to
it that he was 'kept in his place, kept down.' The oppor-
tunistic and compromising position of the Negro as a buffer
between labor and capital came to an end.

The enigma of the 'yellow union,' which in 1919 was
known as the American Unity Packers' Union, and in 1921
as the American Unity Welfare League, furnished the only
element of comedy in the situation. Would the butchers'
union furnish an oxygen tank for it, now that the packers
who had organized their own union had turned it down?
The swan song which its leader published made a futile
bid to attract the notice and commendation of organized
labor.

BLACK AND WHITE STRIKE AT YARDS, STAY AWAY,
NO RACE STRIKE BREAKERS SAFE AT STOCK YARDS.

Two thousand colored men from the American Unity Welfare
League struck with the white union strikers Monday, December
5, and closed Armour's plant in the beef department, killing
floor, and cold storage and loading docks were practically put
out of commission, are the departments in which most of the
colored men are employed. At Swifts most of the same departments were closed down, and the entire hog killing floor was
also closed down.

There has been several agents from Armour and Swift beg-
ging Negroes through the Y.M.C.A. and the Urban League
to take the place of the strikers, but they are not making any
headway because no laborers stop at the Y.M.C.A., and the
American Unity Welfare Union is standing pat with the meat
cutters and will not go to the yards until the packers abolish
the organization that was organized by the packers as we do
not believe that the packers are organizing laborers for the
labor benefit but were organizing them for the packers' benefit
is the reason why we are striking with the white packers.[1]

The Negroes as a group, therefore, lined up with the employers.[2] To infer that a protest was thereby registered
against the unions would be false. Had this been the case,
the efforts of the more radical unions to gain their interest
would have been more successful. The I.W.W. made no
headway with the colored stockyard workers. The packers
offered jobs which were of themselves more important than
any benefits the union might hope to provide, and the Negro
'intellectuals' urged the advantages to be gained from the
employers and the disadvantages of union membership.
They, the packers, the ministers, social workers, lawyers,
doctors, and the like, were more influential in securing jobs
than were the unions. To the Negro leaders, especially the
clergy, the issue became one of race and offered a means
of retaliation against the domination of the white race. As

---

[1] *The Chicago Advocate,* December 10, 1921, p. 1.
[2] The reports of the Negro organizers indicate that in December, 1921, the
membership of Local 651 stood at 112, of whom 49 were in good standing.

the employers turned to the ministry to supply them with laborers, sermons were preached against workers of various nationalities. A strike which resulted in the employment of more Negroes and the crushing of a union which discriminated against them was a victory. Strike-breaking as a means by which the race advanced had been established. By its use a foothold had been gained in the packing industry and further progress would be made. It is true the packers were endeavoring to influence public opinion, but their objective was rather to secure strike-breakers to meet a specific need than to stimulate race antagonism. The Negro 'intellectuals' became the victims of rumors.[1] The Y.M.C.A. and the Y.W.C.A. were said to have been established among the Negroes by the big interests, in order that strike-breakers would be furnished in times of stress; a Y.M.C.A. secretary was reported to be on the packers' payroll. It was stated that the politicians and colored ministers in the Black Belt, who received their support from similar sources, kept the colored workers in submission.[2] The Sunday before the strike was called, fifteen union men attended the fifteen most influential colored churches in the Black Belt. In all but one the ministers read communications from the packers

---

[1] At a public meeting for Negroes at Foresters' Hall, 4358 South State Street, Reverend Charles Dixon, a colored preacher, made definite accusations: '. . . the subsidized Negro preachers and editors take their sermons and articles to the negro Y. M. C. A. to be approved and get money there furnished by the packers for the purpose of having the negroes educated to keep out of labor unions.' *The New Majority*, January 14, 1922, p. 5.

Stories which are still current, boastfully repeated as evidence of the goodwill which existed between the packers and the staff of the various philanthropic and religious organizations functioning among the Negroes, show the more subtle ways in which the employers were influencing the Negro group through its leaders. It is credibly reported that, immediately preceding the strike, one of the leading packers would meet, on various occasions, officials of these organizations. In the midst of a casual conversation, he would ask, 'You think the Negro will stand by us if we have trouble in the yards, don't you?' Upon being assured, he would add, 'You know we always count on the Negro, and would hate to be disappointed in him.' He would then be told that if the Negro race furnished strike-breakers and Negro public opinion supported the packers, a protest would be registered against the current manifestation of trade-unionism in the stockyards, and not against trade-union principles. Nor did the matter end here; he would invariably resume the conversation and reintroduce the subject when future occasion offered itself. He would then remark, 'You were right again. I congratulate you as a Negro and as a leader of your race.'

[2] *The New Majority*, December 10, 1921, p. 12. From 1919 to 1921, frequent mention of the use of the colored Y. M. C. A. and colored ministers by the packers appears in *The Butcher Workman* and *The New Majority*.

urging workmen to disregard the strike order. When, on the following Thursday, a Negro organizer attempted to present the workers' problem to the pastors, he found none at home. Upon inquiry, he was told in each case that the pastor was answering a call to report at Armour and Company.

The strike called December 5, 1921, was broken by the use of Negro strike-breakers, who added to the confusion within the establishments by calling strikes of their own.[1] The Amalgamated Meat Cutters and Butcher Workmen of North America had shown splendid resistance in view of the scab reserves which the packers claimed to have at their command:

Some months ago a representative of the Union, while in the office of Roberts and Oakes, was told that Mr. Hall, Assistant General Superintendent of Armour and Company, had just phoned and urged that concern to have nothing to do with the Union because the big packers had twenty thousand starved negroes available for service.[2]

Agents were sent South for Negroes; 'scouts' and 'runners' for the packers collected them from railroad terminals, street corners, elevated railway stations, and poolrooms. Trucks from the packing companies gathered them in from the streets of the Black Belt and provided free transportation to 'Packingtown.' After nine weeks the union declared [3]

[1] There were rumors of difficulties within the plants such as the following: two Negro strike-breakers killed each other during a quarrel at Armour and Company; smallpox broke out in the yards following the attempt to house colored non-union workers. (*The New Majority*, January 21, 1922, p. 1.) During the strike the chief cause of complaint by both the packers and the union arose from the use of intimidating measures; the families, especially the children of the strikers and strike-breakers, were molested. The A.M.C. and B.W. of N.A. received copies of letters which workers received from the packers urging them to return to work with the promise that 'fifty-fifty-clubs' would be organized. *The Butcher Workman*, December, 1921, p. 2.

[2] *Ibid.*, February, 1922, p. 2.

[3] *Ibid.*, pp. 1-2. The returns of the referendum vote, in which less than 25 per cent of those originally affected participated, showed an overwhelming majority in favor of continuing the strike. The colored organizers and other special organizers for the A.M.C. and B.W. of N.A. in Chicago and elsewhere received notice on February 2, 1922, that their services would not be needed after February 4 because of the result of the strike. Mr. G. W. Reed, of Kansas City, bought a tent and appealed to the national organization to permit him to continue with his work. The organizers as well as the colored men in the ranks of organized labor immediately lost all connection with and A.M.C. and B.W. of N.A.

an end to the strike and told its members to return to their work.[1]

[1] The A.M.C. and B.W. of N.A. started the new year of 1922 with $4,470.81 in cash and Liberty Bonds to the value of $5,150.00 in the treasury. During January the strike donations amounted to $2,592.65, of which $1,959.50 came from their own locals.   On March 31, 1922, the cash balance stood at $2,669.30.   (Financial Report of Secretary-Treasurer, Amalgamated Meat Cutters and Butcher Workmen of North America.'   January-March, 1922.) In comparing the financial report of the fiscal year ending June 30, 1921, with that ending June 30, 1922, the receipts of the latter year were a trifle less than 42 per cent, and the disbursements a trifle less than 41 per cent of the former year.   *Report of Proceedings,* 1922, p. 34.

PART II

A STUDY AND COMPARISON OF WHITE AND NEGRO EMPLOYEES IN TWENTY-FOUR SLAUGHTERING AND MEAT-PACKING ESTABLISHMENTS

CHAPTER IV

EMPLOYMENT CONDITIONS OF WHITE AND NEGRO EMPLOYEES

Promotion

PROMOTION is no more a sure reward of effort in this than in other industries. In fact, the character of the industry sets particular boundaries: first, by its minute division of labor and high percentage of unskilled tasks; second, by its seasonality; and third, by the nationality and race demarcation within it.

The patent reply to inquiries centering about promotion possibilities is that since incentive systems of wage payment are used by the majority of the companies, the question of promotion is now satisfactorily solved. It is asserted that each task carries an equal opportunity for reward of effort by a bonus or premium, even though the hourly rate of wages may vary. But the limits within which the individual is in a position to control his production are narrow. Strange as it may seem, with the exception of promotions to supervisory positions, the most effective opportunities for an advance in wages are in the beef-killing rooms, where division of labor is carried to its highest point. The opportunities are limited in number, but the gain in wage and prestige is substantial. Men are first employed for cleaning, trucking, and 'skinning,' working up to several very skilled positions. 'Skinners' look forward to becoming 'floormen' or 'siders'; an equally important occupation may spur the ambitions of 'splitters,' for the aristocracy of the yards is achieved by those whose strength, skill, and experience enable them to sever the vertebræ from the hips to the chuck. Both Negro and white workmen are employed as 'splitters' and 'floormen,' and are well paid.

Were it not for seasonality,[1] status and security would be within reach of many. Work in the yards has become much more regular, but seasonality has not been eliminated.

[1] See Part I, Chap. I, Sec. III, pp. 9 ff.

It affects status in one of two ways: a complete lay-off may be necessary, and when the worker is rehired, a new wage contract is made; or the worker may be transferred to other tasks for all or part of his time, with a wage adjustment in accordance with the wage-scale of the new task; moreover, when cattle begin to come in and the plant takes on more employees, the worker who has been lucky enough to be kept with a reduction in his wages is not assured of a return to his former wage-level.

The practice of departmental shifting during the slack season in an effort to keep the most efficient employees and to distribute the available work as far as possible changes the racial and nationality composition of departments. This has had to be considered when foremen or superintendents were appointed from various nationality groups. Today it operates to an appreciable degree in establishing the racial composition of plants and in limiting the number of Negroes who can hold minor supervisory positions. In the past, a few Negroes have been put in charge of Negro gangs as recognition of efficiency. This has been satisfactory from the viewpoint of the job's requirements. At the time of the seasonal allocation of workers, however, the presence of Negro foremen has always to be taken into account. In the few cases where white men have been asked to work under Negroes, some refusals have been met with. At present the companies avoid the issue as much as possible by giving Negroes supervisory positions only in rare instances. Negroes have seldom advanced beyond the rank of 'strawboss.' [1]

Since range of employments and of wage-rates are narrower for Negro wage-earners than for white, the opportunity of the former to add a few cents an hour to his rate through promotion is also limited. This handicap is more pronounced for women than for men,[2] and for Negro women

[1] The supervisory positions in the large packing companies in the order of their importance are as follows: superintendent, assistant superintendent, divisional or departmental superintendent, general foreman, foreman, assistant foreman, 'strawboss.' The latter is not on salary, but is a manual laborer who works in the ranks.

[2] Copies of service cards of women employees (see Appendix B) over a number of years indicate the limited opportunities for advancement to positions of authority and responsibility. The records of women remaining over a

than for white, perhaps due to native inertia. Many of the oldest and steadiest women workers, both Negro and white, hold the jobs paying the lowest rate of wages. Departments are large, one foreman or superintendent overseeing several divisions. In only one plant in which women were employed were there foreladies, none of whom was a Negress.[1] The forewomen were directly in charge of the women in their divisions, usually numbering less than fifty, and were in turn responsible to a departmental foreman. Their responsibility was limited; most of them had been advanced from workers' benches. Departments composed entirely of Negro women were in the charge of a white foreman.

Length of Service

The more general figures of labor 'turnover,' so readily obtainable from individual establishments, are valueless for the purpose of this study. All report a high rate, but interpretation of a figure standing at '290 per cent' or '350 per cent' cannot be attempted. Reports from many plants show restlessness. The only employment that is offered to the novice is so disagreeable or distasteful that those who accept it for the first time are frequently the 'down-and-outers.' Work is taken in an emergency until something better turns up. And so tasks are engaged upon reluctantly and the least possible effort expended upon their performance. Likes or dislikes for gang bosses, rather than loyalty and enthusiasm for management, indicate another step in the removal of the worker from a feeling of pride in his product. The ultimate success of the business or the quality of the goods offered the consumer are not the concerns of the stockyard's common laborers.

But despite the unanimous confirmation of high rates of mobility and of labor replacement, the fluctuations are said to take place within a comparatively small area, that is, to

period of years and who therefore may be assumed to be acceptable employees show simply the yearly and cyclical fluctuations of the industry in which they are small cogs. Increases from 30 to 33 or 35 cents an hour are frequent, and a few women receive raises which enable them to earn 40 to 45 cents an hour.

[1] Two establishments include a woman on the Employment Department staff and women nurses frequently serve in the plant hospitals. All Industrial Relations Departments are composed entirely of men.

be highly localized. The great mass of employees remains constant, while a few individuals change rapidly. And, in this industry, the unskilled Negro laborer who performs the disagreeable work and the women are the nucleus of the concentrated phenomenon of turnover. Hired during the busy season to fill the ranks of the unskilled, the women and Negroes are discharged for incompetency, dismissed when work is slack, or leave voluntarily after a few months. About a group of workmen who seem fairly regular and steady, revolve those who come in temporarily when needed. They are thus set apart as a transient group whose turnover rate will of necessity be high. The companies count upon the Negroes as an ever-present group of job-seekers who may always be found loitering at the entrance to the employment office.

The habits, health, and living conditions of the Negro contribute to his high rate of labor mobility. The individual Negro, incompetent, invariably sets the standard by which all Negro workmen are judged. The usual criticism runs similar to that from one of the interviews which follows:

The Negro seems to suffer from the northern climate. He has colds, fevers and tuberculosis. His home is not well heated and he does not seem to eat the right food. He also gets into more trouble than the white man. There are many more sexual irregularities among Negroes than among white workers. He does not seem to know how to live decently and quietly in Chicago and these facts keep him out of the shop a very great deal. Yet the Negroes come back to our plant and stick by us. White people, if they have any ambition, soon find that there is easier work and better pay elsewhere and they soon leave us. Negroes are quite glad to get jobs in any factory.

Women, and in particular Negro women, were complained of everywhere as being the most irregular in attendance, and of holding the shortest service records. Their home conditions, 'loose-living,' frequent attendance at cabarets, in addition to their shiftlessness, were invariably mentioned. While cleaner and less apt to be the victim of social disease than the Negro man, it was the Negro woman who 'beat

everything' for the number of times she was compelled to
go to court, get a divorce, attend marriages and funerals,
and watch over sick children. Many of these accusations,
however, were retracted when an effort was made to gain
definite information. Negro women with long, acceptable
service records were then mentioned. Individuals with high-
school training were cited. But these were the 'exceptions.'
The group of Negro women as a whole was never judged
in the light of the more capable of the race, but by the least
desirable. However, when contrasted with the Negro man,
the Negro woman was said to be superior.

Service records were brought to the investigator's attention. The length of service of *separated* employees presented
a striking contrast to those of the *active* working force, because of the high concentration in turnover. Seasonality
would make the number of long service employees relatively
few, were it not for the custom of laying off the least skilled
employees and those most recently hired.[1] This enables the
companies to keep in their service the more skilled workers,
who not infrequently suffer a reduction of wages by the arrangement, and generally of hours also. For the packers
are interested not merely in eliminating the cost of replacement and training of new workers; they wish also to maintain an *esprit de corps,*[2] and realize that it results from years
of common endeavor and effort by workers and management.
The assumption of all industries is that a worker increases
in value to his organization with his length of service.

One great force is diametrically opposed to the establishment of stability by means of the long service record of
active employees. Speeding-up, which requires of the most
skilled workers a high degree of physical strength and en-
durance and leads to fatigue and overstrain, results in the
forfeiture of their places to younger men before they are old
in years. Division of labor has put a premium upon youth-
ful agility and alertness. And although places may be made

[1] In most firms if an employee is laid off for less than two weeks, the service
record remains unbroken. Lay-offs for a longer period are dealt with in-
dividually.

[2] The packers recognize twenty and thirty-five years of service by awarding
leather medals and publishing the wage-earners' names in their respective
plant publications and Year Books.

for the workers who can no longer keep up with the demands of their jobs, this involves so much humiliation and is so distasteful that old-timers often prefer even less desirable work under new surroundings.

In the absence of comprehensive data for all workers and the difficulty of securing them, the group with the higher rates of turnover was chosen for an examination of length of service. A study of the duration of employment in two of the most unattractive and disagreeable departments, the hog-killing and beef casing, reveals a comparatively long service for those who did not leave almost immediately after entrance.

The hog-killing department does not vary greatly in size from year to year.[1] Records afford data as far back as 1918. From the files of the separated and active employees, the number of new employees hired each year was calculated. The department generally has a working-force of 25 women; in 1923, there were from 30 to 35 workers, and during this year of industrial expansion and heavy Negro migration, the number of accessions rose abnormally and remained higher for the two following years, falling slightly in 1925. During these years there was a steady increase in the employment of Negro women which began during the strike of 1921, when they came in 'through the back door,' and continued until 1926. The active file of this department gives the names and records of 24 women. One Negro woman who started work here in 1917 holds the record for length of service. Four women entered the department in 1919, two in 1920 and 1921, six in 1922, three in 1923, and two in 1924, 1925, and 1926, respectively.

Thirteen women are employed in the beef casing department where all work is performed under repulsive conditions. The work-table of Polish women who cut knots from the casings with surgical scissors does not vary much in personnel from year to year. The women are old, and their work is fairly simple. The Negro women stand all day at the sinks with running water, and inflate, inspect, and grade the casings. This work cannot be performed without train-

[1] See Appendix C for a description of the hog-killing and beef casing departments.

ing and experience. The accession rate in the department was high in 1918. It fell the following year, showed a slight increase in 1922, but was low for the remainder of the period—1923 to 1926. One woman has been employed in the same department since 1916, three since 1918, one woman entered it in 1919, two in 1922, four in 1923, one in 1924 and 1926, respectively.

Work Assignments of White and Negro Employees

Racial considerations largely determine the tasks to which wage-earners are assigned. Labor policy has occasioned the introduction of the Negro man into all departments, but racial preference has prescribed the type and number of tasks he may perform. The fact that the Negro woman is subject to a greater degree of discrimination may be accounted for in two ways. Women are of minor importance to the industry, either as strike-breakers or as producers, for slaughtering and meat-packing is essentially a man's industry. In addition, a high percentage of women employees prepare a finished product for the market, and for this work, which is most open to the comments and criticisms of the public, white women are preferred. Among the countless illustrations of packing-house workers contained in the industry's literature, Negro workmen have been featured as engaged in the making of fertilizer and in the occupations in the hide-cellars.

The type and extent of the preference given the white race in work assignments is shown in the following: In an establishment employing 5,424 at the time of the inquiry, 4,991 were men, of whom 1,519 were Negro and 3,472 white. Of the 433 women employed, 108 were Negro and 325 white. In this plant women were employed because they were considered good strike-breakers and because of the need for nimble fingers. Negro women were especially praised for their loyalty and reliability during labor troubles and for their willingness to do the dirty work which soon became distasteful to foreign women. Three departments refused to employ Negro women: the sliced bacon, oleo, and cheese. When questioned as to the reason, the person interviewed at the plant replied that the women who applied were not fitted for the particular kind of work; that they were the larger, heavier physical types, who handled the knife well and made excellent trimmers or sausage-makers, casing-turners, cleaners, and inspectors. The employment secretary confirmed this, adding that there were Negro women perfectly qualified for the work who did not apply, since the policy of the company was generally known among workers. He searched his experience of twenty years to account for the fact. Negro women had been debarred from the butterine room in order that the question of black hands touching the oleo would not be raised by plant visitors. When the cheese department was established as a division of the oleo room, racial discrimination was extended to it. Sliced bacon is one of the products in which the firm takes great pride; no expense is spared in its manufacture and distribution. Visitors, including all foreign guests and personal friends of the management, are always taken to the room in which the bacon is handled. The walls are painted white and the workers are clad in white. The employment secretary could find no other reason for excluding Negroes than that the picture might seem prettier to visitors if it were all white.

A larger firm employed about 10,000 wage-workers, among whom were 2,113 colored men and 183 colored women. Personnel and employment secretaries and those in charge of various divisions reported that Negro men were not to be found among the skilled mechanics, or in the smokehouse, because the product was considered a 'finished' one. Negro women were excluded from the butterine department because the superintendent said he did not like them. He had once been forced to take them because of a shortage in the labor supply, and they were satisfactory workers, but his preference is for white women. Negro women are also excluded from the pharmaceutical departments and the packing of gut strings. The departments are clean, light, and comfortable, but the work requires no special skill and is not highly paid. In the casing room, where working conditions are poor and wages low, Negro women predominate, having qualified on two scores: first, their physique, and second, their economic status which, according to the employment secretary, puts them 'on their haunches.' Pork trimming, at which foreign women are efficient, requires a considerable degree of physical strength and is one of the best jobs open to women because it is paid on the piece-work basis.

Two establishments within the stockyards dealing in soaps, casings, and fertilizers gave a not uncommon type of interview. In the first instance a summary of notes taken from an interview with the secretary of the company is given; in the second, with the president.

We pay very little attention to the few women in our plant; they just do odd jobs. We keep some all the time and they stay with us pretty steadily. There are thirty Poles and Lithuanians and six colored women, the lowest type in existence. The Poles and Lithuanians do "pick-up work" around the tables, types of sorting and arranging of materials. All six Negro women are on glue stripping, for no other women would do it. Both types of work are very dirty. As we handle tallow, glue, soap and fertilizer, our factory has to be greasy, oily, dirty, and smelly.

The white and Negro women are treated alike and we pay them the same wage, thirty cents an hour. We notice that the Negro men are getting lazy now that the weather is beginning to get warmer. Our plant is never slack and we need workers who are steady. The trouble with the Negro is that he is very lazy. Ambition is entirely lacking. The only way to get work out of him is the way they got it out of him in the South— with a whip. On the other hand, he is so good-natured that you cannot help liking him and getting along with him.

.   .   .   .

We employ about one hundred and fifty in our little concern: one hundred white men, about forty Negroes, and perhaps ten Polish women. We took the Negroes on as strike-breakers in 1921 and have kept them ever since in order to be prepared for any sort of outbreak. We have never been aware of any difficulty between the Negroes and whites in our plant. They work together under identical conditions as to wages and hours of employment.

The women cut and pack the beef. We must be scrupulous along sanitary lines and only white hands are fit to touch the meat. People would not buy our meat if they knew that colored women were employed. If we were a larger plant, we could watch the women more carefully, employing someone who did nothing but supervise them, but we cannot afford that. We could hire Negro women, but their hands would have to be washed almost every hour and we would have to manicure them.

Verbal replies to queries as to work assignments and employment conditions convey information as to attitudes, judgments, and ratings which may be of far greater significance than the facts themselves. The details of each establishment, however, are so complex that the information thus obtained is certain to carry a high degree of error. The following material [1] was secured from the service cards of an independent firm of national importance employing two thousand. Negro men were excluded from employments commercial in character, nor were there any Negro skilled mechanics. Negroes were found in limited numbers in almost every other department and they formed a much higher percentage of the unskilled laborers than did the white men.

Since a greater degree of discrimination was exercised among the women, the study was here pursued with special reference to them. There were on the payroll 247 white and 120 Negro women. With the exception of 24 white women who were piece-workers, all were paid by the hour. The 29 departments and occupations in which women were employed were sliced bacon, sausage manufacture, hair, wool, laboratory, summer sausage, sausage packing, boiled ham packing, ham boiling, beef cutting, lard refining, canning, produce, label department, sheep fat, mutton tallow, beef tallow, beef casing, casing packing, hog-killing, hog head, pork trimming, bone, butterine, smokehouse, printing, laundry, night janitress, and matrons. Three of the departments, the sliced bacon, butterine, and chipped beef had a definite policy against employing Negro women, and despite absence of official objection in other departments,

---

[1] Table I presents a departmental analysis of the plant, and the nationality and race of the women workers. The data are summarized in Chart I showing the hourly rate of wages.

TABLE I. DEPARTMENTAL DISTRIBUTION OF WOMEN EMPLOYEES BY RACE AND NATIVITY, IN A SLAUGHTERING AND MEAT-PACKING ESTABLISHMENT

DEPARTMENT	TOTAL	NATIVE-BORN			FOREIGN-BORN
		Native Parentage		Foreign Parentage	
		White	Negro		
Total...............	367	28	120	50	169
Hair................	30	—	19	3	8
Casing packing......	27	—	18	4	5
Hog-killing.........	24	1	16	—	7
Sausage manufacture.	37	—	11	5	21
Summer sausage.....	64	—	11	6	47
Beef tallow.........	9	—	9	—	—
Beef casing.........	13	—	9	—	4
Mutton tallow.......	8	—	8	—	—
Hog head...........	12	—	4	—	8
Lard refining.......	16	7	4	—	5
Canning............	25	1	4	2	18
Bone...............	3	—	3	—	—
Smokehouse........	7	—	2	4	1
Matrons............	4	1	1	—	2
Sausage packing.....	5	2	1	—	2
Sliced bacon........	34	10	—	12	12
Pork trimming.......	13	—	—	3	10
Night janitress......	5	—	—	—	5
Butterine..........	8	—	—	3	5
Laundry............	5	1	—	—	4
Sheep fat...........	2	—	—	—	2
Printing............	4	—	—	4	—
Label department....	4	1	—	3	—
Produce............	3	3	—	—	—
Laboratory.........	1	1	—	—	—
Boil hams..........	1	—	—	1	—
Beef cutting........	1	—	—	—	1
Boiled ham packing..	1	—	—	—	1
Wool..............	1	—	—	—	1

there was a tendency toward racial segregation in many occupations.

No one assumes responsibility for debarring Negro women from the departments which play a prominent part on the visitors' route throughout the plant, but the public's wishes are said to be of primary consideration. The public dislikes the idea of having Negro women handle food, and if they do, it does not wish to be cognizant of the practice. Visitors comment upon the performance by Negro women of certain tasks in which fat grease and juice touch the hand, and they are said to be responsible for debarring Negro women from the oleo room, although no hands touch the butterine in the course of packing, so skillfully is it performed. The company employs Negro men to pack pails of the same butterine, which not only is shoveled into the receptacle, but must often first be molded by hand into a workable mass. This the public does not see. The firm holds the public responsible also for the debarment of the Negro from the packing of bacon and of chipped beef. It has never tried out the public on this, but does not consider such an experiment worth while. Positions in departments inaccessible to Negroes are at a premium. They constitute the most agreeable tasks open to women employees, under the best conditions of work in the establishment. The work is not skilled, and requires a minimum of training and experience.

The labor performed by women employees may be classified roughly as follows: first, the least attractive work performed by Negro and to a less extent by foreign women in such departments as the beef casing, beef tallow, mutton tallow, hog-killing, casing packing, hog head, bone, and hair. Among the occupations are those of inspecting, washing, grading and measuring casings, cutting bungs, washing chitterlings, packing and trimming fat, trimming lungs, hearts, kidneys, ovaries, paunch, snouts, tongues. Additional tasks are those of splitting heads, cutting ear drums, pulling ruffle fat and mid-guts, weaving and opening ropes, and clipping tails. Second, are those occupations found in departments such as the sausage and canning. Here the work consists in washing, linking, tying, stuffing, hanging, wrapping, and packing sausage, tying and sewing casings, and stuffing, washing, capping, weighing, and packing cans and jars. Few Negro women are employed in a third small group of occupations in which native white women and a few of foreign birth pack, wrap, and label trademarked products for the retail trade.

Estimated Hourly and Weekly Rate of Wages and Hours of Employment of White and Negro Men

Detailed payroll material showing hourly and weekly rates of earnings was sought from only one meat-packing establishment. Additional data are available, however, from the twenty-four which were visited. A warning must precede presentation of the data. A *rate* of wages may not represent the actual amount of money received by anyone. Moreover, the range of median hourly and weekly *rates* indicates only that half of the workmen of each group are paid at a higher rate, half at a lower rate than the amount specified. The figures thus secured are of a subjective nature. Apart from their accuracy, they may be of importance as showing in a study dealing with racial attitudes and preferences what the various persons interviewed thought groups of workers were being paid.

Answers to the *three* questions concerning the hourly rate of wages paid by the twenty-four firms employing 16,727 white and 6,905 Negro workmen were in each case prefaced by a statement to the effect that no discrimination existed in the rate of payment for similar tasks. The beginning and lowest hourly rate of wages offered by the majority of the firms to applicants for unskilled jobs was 40 cents; in a few instances 45 cents was the lowest. Four establishments which employed Negroes exclusively as 'pick-ups' and roustabouts, the 'cheapest work,' reported that no white men, even unskilled, were put upon the payroll at as low a wage as that paid to these colored men. The replies to the query, 'What is the highest hourly rate of wages which your establishment pays to white and colored men?' brought in most cases an explanation that all workers were eligible to the tasks which paid at the rate of 80 to 85 cents. Although some skilled Negroes held such jobs, it was admitted that more white than colored workmen were thus employed. Eight firms reported that colored men were debarred from the tasks for which the highest rates of wages were paid. The establishments whose maximum hourly rate of wages was 75 or 70 cents likewise reported that fewer colored than white men were employed at these rates. Sixty-five and 45 cents were the lowest maximum hourly rates paid by any establishment to white and colored workmen, respectively. Chart II shows the estimated range of median hourly wage-rates. In no instance did the representative of an establishment think that the median hourly rate of its colored workers exceeded 55 cents, and for slightly more than 40 per cent of the white workers, a median hourly rate was thought to be in excess of that amount.

Since 1912 the noticeable stabilization of hours of employment in the meat-packing establishments has resulted in a reduction in the length of the working-day. Swift and Company first guaranteed a 40-hour week to its employees, and in 1913, Morris and Company, Armour and Company, Cudahy and Company, and Wilson and Company did likewise. In 1916, Swift and Company raised the weekly guarantee five hours. In order to secure this 'guaranteed' or 'gang-time,' which was within the reach of only certain workers, employees were required to report each day and perform the full 'gang-time' or other work. The guarantees were usually for 40, 45, or 48 hours pay each week, and the killing, cutting, and lugging gangs were generally included. Between 1918 and 1921, Judge Alschuler again established the 8-hour day in the industry,[1] and the 40-hour guarantee of pay. The latter has been maintained [2] by the leading packers.

White and Negro workers, in a given establishment, were reported as having different scheduled working-hours which were determined by the type of work each performed and

[1] See pp. 39 ff. The 8-hour day had previously been established in 1886. See p. 14.

[2] Companies differ in the administration of the 40-hour guarantee of wage payment, which in no case provides for full-time employment during a given week or on a particular day. The majority maintain that absenteeism does not break the guarantee, which is computed on the basis of the 'gang-time' minus the absent hours. In some companies the guaranteed time is equivalent to 6⅔ hours a day. If the worker does not start on Monday, some companies do not give the guarantee; others compute it on the basis of the 6⅔-hour day. The same rule applies in the case of separations. Tardiness of 15 minutes reduces the weekly guarantee to 39 hours. Overtime, which most companies pay at the rate of time and a half times the regular rate after 55 hours a week or 10 hours in one day, and excess time, may be earned during the same week.

The more reputable companies have taken a stand against the reduction of the payroll at the end of one week, followed by its augmentation at the beginning of the next week. Plants whose guarantee is equivalent to a 6⅔-hour workday make frequent use of this method to eliminate the necessity of paying excess time.

CHART I

HOURLY RATE OF WAGES OF WOMEN EMPLOYEES
IN A MEAT-PACKING ESTABLISHMENT

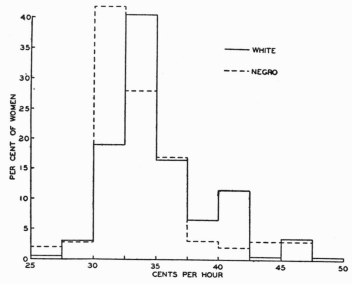

NUMBER AND PER CENT DISTRIBUTION AND CUMULATIVE PERCENTAGES

CENTS PER HOUR	WHITE			NEGRO		
	Number	Per cent Distribution	Cumulative Percentage	Number	Per cent Distribution	Cumulative Percentage
Total..........	223	100.0		120	100.0	
25.00–27.49.....	1	0.4	0.4	2	1.7	1.7
27.50–29.99.....	6	2.7	3.1	3	2.5	4.2
30.00–32.49.....	42	18.8	21.9	50	41.6	45.8
32.50–34.99.....	90	40.4	62.3	34	28.3	74.1
35.00–37.49.....	36	16.2	78.5	20	16.7	90.8
37.50–39.99.....	14	6.3	84.8	3	2.5	93.3
40.00–42.49.....	25	11.2	96.0	2	1.7	95.0
42.50–44.99.....	1	0.4	96.4	3	2.5	97.5
45.00–47.49.....	7	3.2	99.6	3	2.5	100.0
47.50 and over...	1	0.4	100.0	—	—	—

not by their color. In the 'good old days,' following 8 and even 10 hours of killing, cutting, and skinning, several hours of carting, scrubbing, and cleaning up were sometimes added to complete the day's toil. The more menial tasks are today performed by common laborers hired for this express purpose and invariably require longer hours than

TABLE II–A. DAILY HOURS OF WHITE AND NEGRO MEN EM-
PLOYEES IN TWENTY-FOUR SLAUGHTERING AND MEAT-PACK-
ING ESTABLISHMENTS

HOURS PER DAY	TOTAL	WHITE	NEGRO
Total..........................	23,632	16,727	6,905
8..............................	16,593	11,957	4,636
Over 8 and under 9.............	2,467	1,559	908
9..............................	3,586	2,605	981
10.............................	986	606	380

TABLE II–B. PERCENTAGE OF MEN EMPLOYEES OF EACH RACE
WORKING SPECIFIED DAILY HOURS

HOURS PER DAY	TOTAL	WHITE	NEGRO
Total..........................	100.0	100.0	100.0
8..............................	70.2	71.5	67.1
Over 8 and under 9.............	10.4	9.3	13.2
9..............................	15.2	15.6	14.2
10.............................	4.2	3.6	5.5

TABLE II–C. PERCENTAGE OF WHITE AND NEGRO MEN EM-
PLOYEES WORKING SPECIFIED DAILY HOURS

HOURS PER DAY	TOTAL	WHITE	NEGRO
Total..........................	100.0	70.8	29.2
8..............................	100.0	72.1	27.9
Over 8 and under 9.............	100.0	63.2	36.8
9..............................	100.0	72.6	27.4
10.............................	100.0	61.5	38.5

CHART II

'MEDIAN' HOURLY RATE OF WAGES OF MEN EMPLOYEES
IN TWENTY-FOUR SLAUGHTERING AND
MEAT-PACKING ESTABLISHMENTS

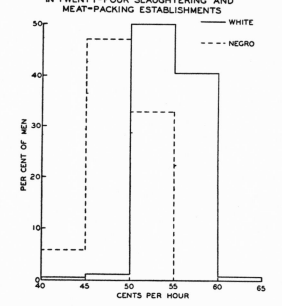

NUMBER AND PER CENT DISTRIBUTION AND CUMULATIVE PERCENTAGES

CENTS PER HOUR	WHITE			NEGRO		
	Number	Per cent Distri- bution	Cumu- lative Percentage	Number	Per cent Distri- bution	Cumu- lative Percentage
Total..........	16,727	100.0		6,905	100.0	
40.00–44.99.....	20	0.1	0.1	397	5.8	5.8
45.00–49.99.....	200	1.2	1.3	3,197	46.3	52.1
50.00–54.99.....	8,312	49.7	51.0	2,253	32.6	84.7
55.00–59.99.....	6,780	40.5	91.5	—	—	84.7
60.00–64.99.....	75	0.5	92.0	—	—	84.7
Not reported....	1,340	8.0	100.0	1,058	15.3	100.0

do the semi-skilled and skilled jobs. Five of the twenty-four establishments had a scheduled working-day (basic or regular full-time) of 10 or more hours; Negro men constituted 29.2 per cent of the workmen in the twenty-four establishments, and 38.5 per cent in the five plants.[1]

Incentive systems of wage payment in the larger packing companies affect weekly wages. One-fourth of both colored and white men were employed by establishments in which the lowest weekly rate of earnings for a Negro man was $15; for a white man, $17. In establishments employing one-fourth more of the laborers of each group, the rate of earnings for common laborers was $22 for a white man, $20 for a Negro. And although a few establishments reported that their maximum weekly rate of earnings was $45, an estimate was made to the effect that one-third of the Negro men and perhaps two-fifths of the white men were working in establishments paying a maximum rate of $35 a week, an amount which was rarely exceeded by a member of either group. While a disparity exists in the average amounts of the weekly rate of earnings of white and Negro workers, the difference is less than that between the hourly rate of wages paid to the workers of the two racial groups. As shown in Chart III the estimated median rate of weekly earnings of 36 per cent of the colored men was within the range of $20 but under $25; the number of white men in jobs which earned as little as this was negligible. The median rate of weekly earnings of the greatest number of workmen in the firms, 50 per cent of the colored and 71.8 per cent of the white, was estimated as falling within the range of $25 but under $30.

Estimated Hourly and Weekly Rate of Wages and Hours of Employment of White and Negro Women

Women had employment in eighteen of the twenty-four establishments. Negro women were either entirely debarred from the departments in which the more agreeable conditions of employment were found or their entrance was lim-

---

[1] The facts pertaining to the daily and weekly hours of the two groups of men in the twenty-four establishments are shown in Tables II–A, II–B, II–C, and Tables III–A, III–B, and III–C.

CHART III

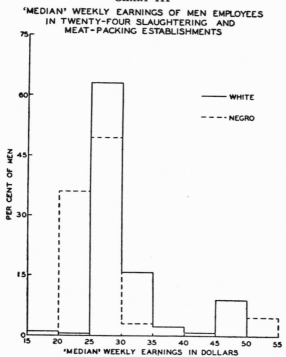

'MEDIAN' WEEKLY EARNINGS OF MEN EMPLOYEES IN TWENTY-FOUR SLAUGHTERING AND MEAT-PACKING ESTABLISHMENTS

NUMBER AND PER CENT DISTRIBUTION AND CUMULATIVE PERCENTAGES

'MEDIAN' WEEKLY EARNINGS	WHITE			NEGRO		
	Number	Per cent Distri-bution	Cumu-lative Percentage	Number	Per cent Distri-bution	Cumu-lative Percentage
Total..........	16,727	100.0		6,905	100.0	
$15.00–$19.99...	100	0.6	0.6	—	—	—
20.00– 24.99...	20	0.1	0.7	2,488	36.0	36.0
25.00– 29.99...	12,013	71.8	72.5	3,452	50.0	86.0
30.00– 34.99...	2,652	15.9	88.4	175	2.5	88.5
35.00– 39.99...	330	2.0	90.4	—	—	88.5
40.00– 44.99...	20	0.1	90.5	3	0.1	88.6
45.00– 49.99...	1,472	8.8	99.3	—	—	88.6
50.00– 54.99...	—	—	99.3	329	4.8	93.4
Not reported...	120	0.7	100.0	458	6.6	100.0

TABLE III–A. HOURS PER WEEK OF WHITE AND NEGRO MEN
EMPLOYEES IN TWENTY-FOUR SLAUGHTERING AND MEAT-
PACKING ESTABLISHMENTS

HOURS PER WEEK	TOTAL	WHITE	NEGRO
Total........................	23,632	16,727	6,905
Under 44......................	1,044	757	287
44............................	9,843	7,473	2,370
Over 44 and under 48...........	715	255	460
48............................	7,458	5,031	2,427
50............................	3,586	2,605	981
55............................	936	581	355
60............................	50	25	25

TABLE III–B. PERCENTAGE OF MEN EMPLOYEES OF EACH RACE
WORKING SPECIFIED WEEKLY HOURS

HOURS PER WEEK	TOTAL	WHITE	NEGRO
Total........................	100.0	100.0	100.0
Under 44......................	4.4	4.5	4.2
44............................	41.6	44.7	34.3
Over 44 and under 48...........	3.0	1.5	6.7
48............................	31.6	30.1	35.1
50............................	15.2	15.6	14.2
55............................	4.0	3.5	5.1
60............................	0.2	0.1	0.4

TABLE III–C. PERCENTAGE OF WHITE AND NEGRO MEN EM-
PLOYEES WORKING SPECIFIED WEEKLY HOURS

HOURS PER WEEK	TOTAL	WHITE	NEGRO
Total........................	100.0	70.8	29.2
Under 44......................	100.0	72.5	27.5
44............................	100.0	75.9	24.1
Over 44 and under 48...........	100.0	35.7	64.3
48............................	100.0	67.5	32.5
50............................	100.0	72.6	27.4
55............................	100.0	62.1	37.9
60............................	100.0	50.0	50.0

CHART IV

'MEDIAN' HOURLY RATE OF WAGES OF WOMEN EMPLOYEES
IN EIGHTEEN SLAUGHTERING AND
MEAT-PACKING ESTABLISHMENTS

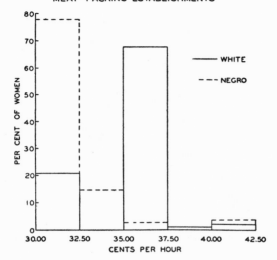

NUMBER AND PER CENT DISTRIUBTION AND CUMULATIVE PERCENTAGES

CENTS PER HOUR	WHITE			NEGRO		
	Number	Per cent Distri-bution	Cumu-lative Percentage	Number	Per cent Distri-bution	Cumu-lative Percentage
Total..........	3,111	100.0		1,126	100.0	
30.00–32.49.....	662	21.3	21.3	894	79.4	79.4
32.50–34.99.....	—	—	—	173	15.4	94.8
35.00–37.49.....	2,233	71.8	93.1	27	2.4	97.2
37.50–39.99.....	45	1.4	94.5	—	—	—
40.00–42.49.....	59	1.9	96.4	32	2.8	100.0
Not reported....	112	3.6	100.0	—	—	—

ited. They worked at the lowest paid 'blind-alley' jobs in the yards; 25 and 27 cents an hour were not unknown rates of remuneration. Fewer of them than of any other group ever receive promotion, either in transfer to more pleasant surroundings or in an increased wage-rate. Very few women of either group are employed at tasks which carry a wage-rate as high as 45 cents an hour.[1]

The scheduled hours representing the normal full-time working-day or week for women are affected, as in the case of men, by operation of the 40-hour guarantee of pay. The scheduled times of beginning and stopping in all but two establishments were reported as identical for women of both races. In these two cases difference in work assignments occasioned the disparity. Tables IV–A, IV–B, IV–C, and Tables V–A, V–B, V–C show that 41.1 per cent of all the women were working in establishments which operated on a 44-hour weekly schedule; 58.8 per cent in establishments with a scheduled work-day of 8 hours. White women, however, composed 86 per cent and 80 per cent, respectively, of the total number of women in each group. It will be recalled that the white women constituted approximately three-fourths (73.4 per cent), and the Negro women one-fourth (26.6 per cent) of the women wage-earners. More than one-third of the Negro women worked in establishments having a scheduled 9-hour day and 50-hour week.

Chart V shows that the estimated median weekly earnings of the Negro women fell below those of the white women. In spite of the higher rate of wages of the latter, the result of the longer schedule of daily and weekly hours worked by the Negro women is that their total earnings compare favorably with those of the white.

Average Weekly Earnings of Men and Women Employees from 1922 to 1926

In order to secure a check for the estimated weekly rate of earnings, additional data showing average weekly earnings were obtained from payrolls. The maximum number of establishments from which data were obtained for the

[1] See Chart IV for Median Hourly Rate of Wages of Women Employees.

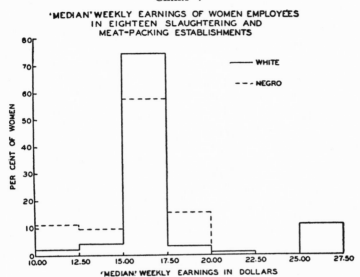

CHART V

'MEDIAN' WEEKLY EARNINGS OF WOMEN EMPLOYEES
IN EIGHTEEN SLAUGHTERING AND
MEAT-PACKING ESTABLISHMENTS

NUMBER AND PER CENT DISTRIBUTION AND CUMULATIVE PERCENTAGES

'MEDIAN' WEEKLY EARNINGS	WHITE			NEGRO		
	Number	Per cent Distribution	Cumulative Percentage	Number	Per cent Distribution	Cumulative Percentage
Total..........	3,111	100.0		1,126	100.0	
$10.00–$12.49...	75	2.4	2.4	135	12.0	12.0
12.50– 14.99...	110	3.5	5.9	114	10.1	22.1
15.00– 17.49...	2,459	79.0	84.9	695	61.7	83.8
17.50– 19.99...	87	2.8	87.7	182	16.2	100.0
20.00– 22.49...	30	1.0	88.7	—	—	—
22.50– 24.99...	—	—	88.7	—	—	—
25.00– 27.49...	350	11.3	100.0	—	—	—

TABLE IV–A. DAILY HOURS OF WHITE AND NEGRO WOMEN EMPLOYEES IN EIGHTEEN SLAUGHTERING AND MEAT-PACKING ESTABLISHMENTS

HOURS PER DAY	TOTAL	WHITE	NEGRO
Total	4,237	3,111	1,126
8	2,490	1,992	498
Over 8 and under 9	579	390	189
9	1,074	670	404
10	94	59	35

TABLE IV–B. PERCENTAGE OF WOMEN EMPLOYEES OF EACH RACE WORKING SPECIFIED DAILY HOURS

HOURS PER DAY	TOTAL	WHITE	NEGRO
Total	100.0	100.0	100.0
8	58.8	64.0	44.2
Over 8 and under 9	13.7	12.5	16.8
9	25.3	21.6	35.9
10	2.2	1.9	3.1

TABLE IV-C. PERCENTAGE OF WHITE AND NEGRO WOMEN EMPLOYEES WORKING SPECIFIED DAILY HOURS

HOURS PER DAY	TOTAL	WHITE	NEGRO
Total	100.0	73.4	26.6
8	100.0	80.0	20.0
Over 8 and under 9	100.0	67.4	32.6
9	100.0	62.4	37.6
10	100.0	62.8	37.2

period was ten; the minimum, six. The maximum number of men for whom wage data were computed was 19,446; the minimum, 7,576; the maximum and minimum number of women employed in the establishments was 2,885 and 929, respectively. The racial composition of wage-earners is un-

TABLE V–A. HOURS PER WEEK OF WHITE AND NEGRO WOMEN EMPLOYEES IN EIGHTEEN SLAUGHTERING AND MEAT-PACKING ESTABLISHMENTS

HOURS PER WEEK	TOTAL	WHITE	NEGRO
Total............................	4,237	3,111	1,126
Under 44........................	250	109	141
44..............................	1,741	1,498	243
Over 44 and under 48...........	66	60	6
48..............................	1,012	715	297
50..............................	1,074	670	404
55..............................	94	59	35

TABLE V–B. PERCENTAGE OF WOMEN EMPLOYEES OF EACH RACE WORKING SPECIFIED WEEKLY HOURS

HOURS PER WEEK	TOTAL	WHITE	NEGRO
Total............................	100.0	100.0	100.0
Under 44........................	5.9	3.5	12.5
44..............................	41.1	48.2	21.6
Over 44 and under 48...........	1.6	1.9	0.5
48..............................	23.9	23.0	26.4
50..............................	25.3	21.5	35.9
55..............................	2.2	1.9	3.1

TABLE V–C. PERCENTAGE OF WHITE AND NEGRO WOMEN EMPLOYEES WORKING SPECIFIED WEEKLY HOURS

HOURS PER WEEK	TOTAL	WHITE	NEGRO
Total............................	100.0	73.4	26.6
Under 44........................	100.0	43.6	56.4
44..............................	100.0	86.0	14.0
Over 44 and under 48...........	100.0	90.9	9.1
48..............................	100.0	70.7	29.3
50..............................	100.0	62.4	37.6
55..............................	100.0	62.8	37.2

known.   Since 1922 and the early months of 1923, there
has been a gradual increase in the average weekly earnings
of both men and women employees.   In 1926, the average
weekly earnings ranged from $26 to $28.34 for men and
from $18.19 to $20.13 for women.[1]

[1] See *Bulletin of the United States Bureau of Labor Statistics*, No. 373, 1923,
and No. 421, 1925: 'Wages and Hours of Labor in the Slaughtering and
Meat-Packing Industry.'

PART III

A STUDY AND COMPARISON OF WHITE AND
NEGRO EMPLOYEES IN A TYPICAL
MEAT-PACKING ESTABLISHMENT

CHAPTER V

ANALYSIS OF EMPLOYEES BY RACE AND SEX
FROM 1922 TO 1926

Fluctuations in Employment

THE progress, position, and efficiency of Negroes as workmen, and the operation of racial factors in the slaughtering and meat-packing industry will next be viewed from the standpoint of the experience of a single typical establishment. Absence of many data on the subject determined the procedure—a statistical analysis and interpretation of the data taken from the official records of one company, chosen because of the management's coöperation and interest. This was supplemented by statements based upon the personal impressions of company officials. The comparison of the two racial groups by sex will include a consideration of their relative numerical importance, wage-rates, weekly and daily hours of employment, weekly and premium earnings, and labor turnover.

The company officials, including the president, vice-president, superintendent, employment secretary, and foremen, maintained that the personnel and employment policies were free from racial prejudice. In more than twenty years, policy in respect of employing Negro and white workers has not changed. As an illustration the following procedure was cited: when workers are needed in a department, the foreman sends to the employment office for the required number, not designating whether colored or white laborers are to be sent.[1] Old employees are given preference in the employment office, but other than this each applicant is judged on the basis of experience and fitness for the opening. Negroes were introduced as strike-breakers in 1894 and used in large numbers in 1904 and 1921. As they came

[1] This statement, made by the employment secretary and general superintendent, was contradicted by foremen, who asserted that they made use of the opportunity to indicate a racial preference provided on the requisition slip for unskilled labor.

97

into the various departments, the general superintendent instructed the foremen that no color line was to be drawn and they took their places by the side of white wage-earners throughout the plant; nor was special provision made for them in restroom, cloakroom, or restaurant accommodations. Nevertheless, because of the 'unreliability, unsteadiness, and inefficiency' of the Negroes, a preference for white workers was expressed.

The employment secretary questions each worker who leaves the plant as to the cause. He recalls no case of one who was discharged or who left voluntarily for a reason which might be attributed to racial antagonism. White and Negro wage-earners in charge of particular gangs or operations teach each other their work. This is accepted without comment or complaint. Interviews with workmen did not produce evidence of marked racial antipathies.[1]

The plant records found under the general heading of the *Labor Analysis* were invaluable, and material from them appears in this and subsequent chapters. Extending over a four-year period, November 25, 1922, to November 20, 1926, inclusive, the information consisted of a weekly record of all employees by race and by sex, an estimate of the number of applicants at the hiring station and those hired, by race. The accessions and separations were classified by race and sex. The length of service of those who left and the reasons for leaving were given. From these data, graphically presented in Chart VI, a downward trend of employment is apparent for the period as a whole. Nineteen hundred and twenty-three was a year of general prosperity in which this industry participated; 1924, one of depression ᵀʰe decrease in employment continued in 1925 and 1926, culminating in a severe period of unemployment in 1927.[2] Never since

[1] As proof of the absence of racial antagonisms, many accounts were heard of the ball-game incident described on p. 50.

[2] Illinois Department of Labor, *The Labor Bulletin*, 'Course of Employment in Selected Industries,' June, 1928, p. 191. Index numbers of employment and of payrolls in the slaughtering and meat-packing industry are presented in Table 9, p. 46, *Bulletin of the United States Bureau of Labor Statistics*, No. 472. The 1923 average number of employees and the 1923 average amount of payrolls were taken as the base or 100 per cent. Index numbers by years were: Employment, 100 in 1923, 93.7 in 1924, 85 in 1925, 81.4 in 1926, and 81 in 1927; and the payrolls were 100 in 1923, 94.4 in 1924, 86.7 in 1925, 84.5 in 1926, and 84.4 in 1927. During the period July, 1922, to

CHART VI

TOTAL EMPLOYEES,
AND RATIOS OF WHITE AND NEGRO EMPLOYEES BY SEX.
DATA PLOTTED BY WEEKS, NOVEMBER 25, 1922 – NOVEMBER 27, 1926

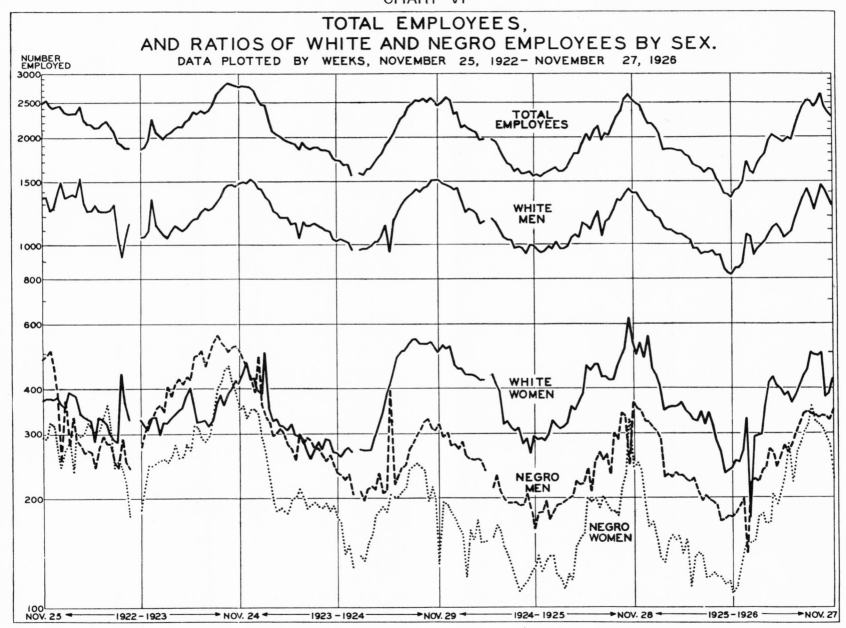

1923, during peak or slack periods, has the number of workers equaled those employed in that year. Moreover, seasonality increased. In 1923, almost two-thirds (65.5 per cent) as many workers were employed during the slack period as during the busy; in 1926, a few more than half (51.4 per cent).[1] The percentage of men and women on the plant payroll has varied but slightly: each year within the range of the study, over 70 per cent of the employees were men. It will be seen from Chart VII that the variations occurring in the racial composition of the total working unit were the result of dissimilar changes within the sex groups. The extent of these variations and to what causes they were attributable will constitute the first step in examining the status of the Negro workman.

Comparison of Tables VII, VIII, IX, and X shows that the fluctuations in employment of white and Negro men and women present striking differences. Chart VI shows that in the case of white men the percentages of the total number of employees which they constituted were fairly uniform throughout the four-year period. Their fluctuations corresponded regularly with the seasonal trend. The similarity in the flux is so striking that no significant change in policy concerning their employment could have been

TABLE VI. SEASONAL FLUCTUATION OF EMPLOYEES IN A MEAT-PACKING ESTABLISHMENT, 1922 TO 1926

YEAR	MAXIMUM NUMBER[c]	MINIMUM NUMBER[c]	PER CENT MINIMUM FORMS OF MAXIMUM
1922[a]	2,530	—	—
1923	2,816	1,845	65.5
1924	2,573	1,574	61.2
1925	2,609	1,558	59.7
1926[b]	2,625	1,348	51.4

[a] The data are for the last six weeks of 1922.
[b] The data are for the first eleven months of 1926.
[c] The data show the maximum and minimum number of employees, by weeks, respectively.

August, 1928, both monthly employment and payrolls were highest (107.9 and 109.6), respectively, in December, 1923, and lowest (76.2 and 78.1), in April, 1926.

[1] Extremes in fluctuation from 1922 to 1926 are shown in Table VI.

CHART VII

TOTAL EMPLOYEES IN A MEAT-PACKING ESTABLISHMENT,
BY RACE AND SEX

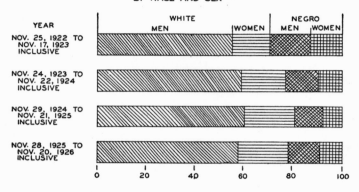

PER CENT DISTRIBUTION

YEAR	TOTAL	WHITE		NEGRO	
		Men	Women	Men	Women
Nov. 25, 1922, to Nov. 17, 1923, Inclusive............	100.0	54.8	15.5	16.6	13.1
Nov. 24, 1923, to Nov. 22, 1924, Inclusive............	100.0	58.4	18.0	13.5	10.1
Nov. 29, 1924, to Nov. 21, 1925, Inclusive............	100.0	59.1	20.4	12.0	8.5
Nov. 28, 1925, to Nov. 20, 1926, Inclusive............	100.0	57.9	19.2	13.2	9.7

inaugurated. The outstanding fact revealed by the study of this establishment stands forth in this connection, namely, the constant ratio maintained between the total number of employees and of white workmen.

The number of Negro men on the company's payroll does not bear a constant relationship to the total number of employees. A strike had been broken during the first month of 1922 by the introduction of Negro strike-breakers. Since 1923, when Negro men at one time constituted 21.8 per cent of the working force, and on eight different occasions reached a weekly ratio of as high as 20 per cent, and on only two occasions fell below 12 per cent, the number of

TABLE VII. EXTREMES IN SEASONAL FLUCTUATION OF WHITE MEN IN A MEAT-PACKING ESTABLISHMENT, 1922 TO 1926

YEAR	MAXIMUM NUMBER	PER CENT OF TOTAL EMPLOYEES	MINIMUM NUMBER	PER CENT OF TOTAL EMPLOYEES	PER CENT MINIMUM FORMS OF MAXIMUM
1922[a]	1,496	60.9	—	—	—
1923	1,534	55.7	927	48.7	60.4
1924	1,506	59.3	962	48.7	63.9
1925	1,450	61.8	952	60.5	65.7
1926[b]	1,472	56.1	817	60.6	55.5

[a] The data are for the last six weeks of 1922.
[b] The data are for the first eleven months of 1926.

TABLE VIII. EXTREMES IN SEASONAL FLUCTUATION OF NEGRO MEN IN A MEAT-PACKING ESTABLISHMENT, 1922 TO 1926

YEAR	MAXIMUM NUMBER	PER CENT OF TOTAL EMPLOYEES	MINIMUM NUMBER	PER CENT OF TOTAL EMPLOYEES	PER CENT MINIMUM FORMS OF MAXIMUM
1922[a]	512	20.8	—	—	—
1923	561	21.3	242	12.9	43.1
1924	364[c]	14.7	198	12.5	54.4
1925	369	14.6	165	10.4	44.7
1926[b]	351	15.3	140	8.3	39.9

[a] The data are for the last six weeks of 1922.
[b] The data are for the first eleven months of 1926.
[c] It is recorded that 398 Negro men were employed the week of August 30, 1924. This number, which was the maximum for the year, was rejected because it represents an isolated and unusual occurrence.

TABLE IX. Extremes in Seasonal Fluctuation of White
Women in a Meat-Packing Establishment, 1922 to 1926

Year	Maximum Number	Per Cent of Total Employees	Minimum Number	Per Cent of Total Employees	Per Cent Minimum Forms of Maximum
1922[a]	380	15.6	—	—	—
1923	477	17.3	286	15.5	60.0
1924	550	21.9	257	13.8	46.7
1925	624	23.9	267	16.9	42.8
1926[b]	503	19.8	177	11.1	35.2

[a] The data are for the last six weeks of 1922.
[b] The data are for the first eleven months of 1926.

TABLE X. Extremes in Seasonal Fluctuation of Negro
Women in a Meat-Packing Establishment, 1922 to 1926

Year	Maximum Number	Per Cent of Total Employees	Minimum Number	Per Cent of Total Employees	Per Cent Minimum Forms of Maximum
1922[a]	344	14.0	—	—	—
1923	472	16.8	179	9.5	37.9
1924	295	11.9	131	8.3	44.4
1925	329	12.6	112	7.0	34.0
1926[b]	360	14.1	111	8.2	30.8

[a] The data are for the last six weeks of 1922.
[b] The data are for the first eleven months of 1926.

Negro men has steadily decreased. Both their number and
the percentage which they constitute of total employees have
decreased for the periods of maximum and of minimum
employment. Moreover, when work is not plentiful, more
colored than white workers lose their jobs. In 1923, one
isolated fact of considerable importance was recorded which
has not been repeated except on rare, brief, and isolated
occasions: for over half the year (29 weeks) more Negro
men were employed than white women.

The firm has become accustomed to the irregularity of
service of its women employees, especially in the case of
Negro women. For our purpose, the facts of greatest significance were the appreciable augmentation in the number

of white women which began in 1923, corresponding with increases in all groups of workers, but continued only in the case of the white women, and the reduction in the number of Negro men and women which began in 1924. At the beginning of 1924, Negro men and white women were employed in almost equal numbers. Within six months the number of Negro men and women and their percentage of the total labor force was reduced; the number of white women and their percentage of the total labor force was increased. Nevertheless, if we compare year by year, the percentage of Negro women to total employees remained nearly constant for the peak and for the slack periods, although in the latter they suffer more than any other group from seasonal unemployment. Approximately one-third are thrown out of work each year when packing is curtailed.

In spite of the assertions of no racial discrimination, the variations from 1922 to 1926 in the number of workers of each group show preference for white labor. Without eliminating Negro labor, each opportunity provided by the state of the labor market was seized to increase the number of white workmen. A brief resume of the facts presented indicates that Negro workmen, whose numbers had been increased in the plant during the strike of December, 1921, and January, 1922, secured additional places in 1923. Prosperity and industrial opportunities curtailed the packers' white labor supply in that year and increased their colored. The 1924 period of acute unemployment enabled employers to discriminate in the choice of employees; Negroes were laid off and the percentage of white labor increased. Seasonal employment, which releases from one-third to one-half of the plant's workers each year, creates a condition utilized to control the selection of labor.

Applicants and Accessions of Employees by Race

Disregarding, for the present, such factors as the desirability of the work, the immigration situation, labor policies, and the social, racial, and economic influences affecting the number of laborers who secure work, attention will be centered on the applicants. How many, both white and Negro, come to the yards seeking employment, and how many are successful? Unfortunately the *Labor Analysis* data were not complete: the number of applicants for positions at the hiring station and the accessions to the payroll were listed by race, but not by sex. The figures must further be discounted because of the recording method used. They do not represent the number who file written applications for work, but are an estimate made once a day by the employment secretary, who has been in charge of the work for over twenty years.

In the absence of great industrial prosperity, the packers have an easy labor market, if quantity is the criterion. Rumor and the knowledge of the hundreds of jobs which have been specialized to facilitate the dismembering of cattle bring hordes of applicants to the hiring station. Failure to secure work elsewhere does not eliminate the possibility of the yards, where in the past a job could usually be 'scabbed.' Everyone feels competent to qualify as an experienced worker in the category of common laborers. And although from year to year more white workmen than Negro are included among the total employees, other questions concerning the number of applicants of each racial group must be considered. To what extent has the change in number in any one racial group been an indication of a scarcity of members of that group available for work at a given time? Was one race substituted for another because of a deficiency of applicants, or in spite of it? Were all available white men and women hired before Negro men and women were taken on? Do the changes occurring in the percentages of total employees of any one group correspond with the number of that particular group which applies for work? Is an applicant of one of these groups rendered fit or unfit by the possession of a particular skill, natural aptitude, or training? Is the racial composition of the employees affected by health considerations? The last query will be dealt with first.

The physician who heads the medical staff of the company has a service record covering fifteen years. The examination which is given before an applicant is accepted for work is the entrance examination to the Employee Benefit Association as well as to the plant. For men, it is thorough for heart and for hernia; for women, for heart and 'general appearance.' The doctor, who is ever on the alert for all suspicious cases of venereal disease, feels that he is quite successful in catching them. If there is any question in the doctor's mind in regard to the male applicant, he must strip for the examination. Moreover, since the foremen have been instructed to watch the health of the workers and to be on the lookout for syphilis and gonorrhea, they not uncommonly report cases for reëxamination.

Since the emphasis which the company places upon health standards has received a considerable amount of publicity among packing house workers, many men about the stock-yards know that it would be useless to apply for work. Fifteen years ago the number turned away because of syphilis was described by the doctor as 'enormous.' Today the number of rejections for this cause is comparatively small; in fact, it does not appear at all during some weeks. It is always higher for the Negro applicants than for the white. The reduction in the number of rejections he does not attribute to the existence of fewer diseased men, but to the selective process which has been set in operation, curtailing an undesirable group of applicants.[1] The smaller percentage of Negro applicants accepted for work is not accounted for solely on the basis of physical disabilities by either the plant physician or the employment secretary. The latter also denies that particular skill, natural aptitude, or training may in turn fit or render unfit the applicants of one of these groups. With almost no exceptions men and women hired for the first time are assigned to tasks requiring no experience or special skill. During the seasonal slack period of employment in the late spring and summer, an effort is made to keep the most competent and skilled by giving them semi-skilled or unskilled work; the poorer and unskilled are laid off. In the autumn, the personnel is built up to handle the large 'run of cattle.' The skilled

[1] For a discussion of Negro health see (1) H. L. Harris, Jr., 'Report on a Negro Health Survey and the Recommendations of the Advisory Committee to the Commissioner of Health, City of Chicago, 1927'; (2) Department of Health, City of Chicago, *Report* for 1923, 1924, 1925, p. 171; (3) H. L. Harris, Jr., 'Negro Mortality Rates in Chicago,' *The Social Service Review*, March, 1927, pp. 58-77.

seek their original tasks; common laborers fill up the vacancies. Moreover, former employees who have been laid off are given preference in obtaining the positions requiring more skill and paying the higher rates of wages.

The employment manager spoke of another factor influencing the number who apply for work. News travels quickly among packing house workers, especially in regard to lay-offs. During slack seasons, for instance, when Negro workmen may be in desperate need of a few days' employment, few come to the yards to ask for it. The longer the period of unemployment, the fewer the applicants. Moreover, by some mysterious means they seem to ascertain what percentage of their number who apply is successful in securing work, and to present themselves in fairly regular proportion to this number. Among Negroes the employment manager seemed conscious of 'hangers-on,' actual applicants or not, who could be secured at a moment's notice. This was not the case with white workers.

An examination of Table XI, giving the number of applicants and accessions recorded for the four-year period, shows two types of variation which relate to the fluctuation of the total number of applicants and to the variation within the racial groups themselves. The total number of applicants was greatest in 1924—18,577—and least in 1926, when there were only 11,595. In 1925, the figure stood at 17,442. During the first and last years within the range of the study, decidedly fewer applicants were recorded than during the second and third years. This fluctuation has already been explained as resulting from the general condition of industry.

But whereas the Negro workmen who sought packing house jobs varied slightly in number between 1923, when industrial employment was plentiful, and 1924, when it was scarce, the percentage which they formed of the total applicants in the yards fell from 64.7 to 45.1. It follows that the inverse is true of white applicants, who increased 123.8 per cent in one year because of the severe industrial depression which made employment scarce elsewhere. And not only did the number of white applicants increase; the percentage

TABLE XI. APPLICANTS AND ACCESSIONS IN A MEAT-PACKING ESTABLISHMENT, NOVEMBER 25, 1922, TO NOVEMBER 20, 1926, INCLUSIVE; NUMBER AND PER CENT DISTRIBUTION

YEAR	APPLICANTS						ACCESSIONS					
	Total		White		Negro		Total		White		Negro	
	Number	Per cent Distribution	Number	Per cent Distribution	Number	Per cent Distribution	Number	Per cent Distribution	Number	Per cent Distribution	Number	Per cent Distribution
November 25, 1922, to November 17, 1923, inclusive	12,927	100.0	4,560	35.3	8,367	64.7	7,153	100.0	3,920	54.8	3,233	45.2
November 24, 1923, to November 22, 1924, inclusive	18,577	100.0	10,205	54.9	8,372	45.1	4,207	100.0	3,340	79.4	867	20.6
November 29, 1924, to November 21, 1925, inclusive	17,442	100.0	11,004	63.1	6,438	36.9	3,550	100.0	2,744	77.3	806	22.7
November 28, 1925, to November 20, 1926, inclusive	11,595	100.0	7,309	63.0	4,286	37.0	3,801	100.0	2,725	71.7	1,076	28.3

they formed of total applicants rose from 35.3 in 1923, to 54.9 in 1924, 63.1 in 1925, and continued at 63 in 1926.

The consequence of the fluctuation in the number of applicants of the two racial groups is clearly reflected in the number of each group which was hired. During 1923, when the labor market was 'tight' and many Negroes were added to the plant force, one-third (35.3 per cent) of the applicants and more than one-half (54.8 per cent) of those who were hired were white. In 1924, more than one-half (54.9 per cent) of the applicants and almost four-fifths (79.4 per cent) of the accessions were white. In 1925 and 1926, the trend in the number and percentages of applicants and accessions by race followed that of 1924, and nothing appeared worthy of special note.

The situation may be viewed from a slightly different angle. According to the records of the company, there were several instances in 1923 of every applicant being hired; the employment secretary was unaware of additional available white laborers. During 24 weeks of the year, more than 90 per cent of the white applicants were accepted. Excluding this same year, if allowance is made for the fact that the data in Table XI are not classified by sex, it will be seen that the labor force could have been maintained by hiring from one-half to one-third of the white applicants. On the basis solely of the number of workers necessary to operate the establishment, the Negro need never have been employed after 1923. Some Negro workmen are almost certain to find employment, and the ratio which this number bears to the total plant force seems to have become fairly constant and well defined. During one week of the four-year period, less than 5 per cent of the white applicants secured employment; the same percentage of successful Negro applicants was recorded for 23 weeks. From 5 to 9.9 per cent of the white and Negro applicants secured employment during 11 and 47 weeks, respectively. One-half or more of the Negro applicants secured employment during 29 weeks; for more than one-third (75 weeks) of the period one-half or more of the white applicants were hired.

The first conclusion as to the status of the Negro workmen in the establishment, namely, that they constitute a separate and distinct labor group, is strongly substantiated by the foregoing analysis. Their employment is held in check within the limits prescribed by the employers' preferences, ratings, and interests. These considerations have established their numerical position within the total labor force and have dictated to what degree Negroes will have success in obtaining employment. In brief, preference for white workmen has been strongly evidenced. The Negro man or woman experiences greater difficulty than does the white in securing a job in the meat-packing establishment.

CHAPTER VI

EMPLOYMENT CONDITIONS OF WHITE AND NEGRO EMPLOYEES

As the third step in establishing the Negro's progress as a laborer, his working conditions, length of working-day, and earnings will be considered in the light of information received from the one selected establishment. Not having definite and accurate information available, the company opened its files, the payroll, and service cards of wage-earners. The week of June 12, 1926, was selected as the date about which the study should revolve because the wage-earners employed at that time were the more regular and reliable of the working force, since they were being retained during the annual slack season. During this week the plant had on its payroll 1,227 employees for whom complete enough data were available for tabulation. The white wage-earners numbered 984, the Negro, 293; of the former group, 743 (58.2 per cent) were men, 241 (18.9 per cent) were women; of the latter, 170 (13.3 per cent) were men, 123 (9.6 per cent) were women. Of 29 nationalities, nine of which had only one representative, the three largest groups were the American-born white (31.4 per cent), the Negro (22.4 per cent), and the Polish laborers (20.5 per cent).[1]

Occupational Distribution, Rate of Wages, Hours of Employment, Weekly Earnings, and Premiums of Men Employees.

Of the 913 men employed in the establishment, about four-fifths (81.4 per cent) of the group were white and one-fifth (18.6 per cent) Negro. The proportion of Negroes who worked as semi-skilled mechanics, as freezers, in two divisions of the tin shop, in the pickle-cellar, and smoke-house, was small. In proportion to the number on the pay-

---

[1] The establishment makes no particular effort to secure accurate data on this subject. New employees designate their nationality or race, and from this record the estimate was made.

CHART VIII

HOURLY RATE OF WAGES OF MEN EMPLOYEES
IN A MEAT-PACKING ESTABLISHMENT

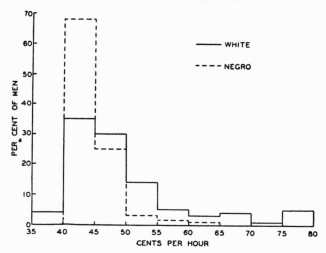

NUMBER AND PER CENT DISTRIBUTION AND CUMULATIVE PERCENTAGES

CENTS PER HOUR	WHITE			NEGRO		
	Number	Per cent Distri- bution	Cumu- lative Percentage	Number	Per cent Distri- bution	Cumu- lative Percentage
Total.........	645	100.0		159	100.0	
Under 40.00.....	23	3.6	3.6	—	—	—
40.00–44.99.....	226	35.0	38.6	109	68.6	68.6
45.00–49.99.....	197	30.5	69.1	41	25.8	94.4
50.00–54.99.....	95	14.7	83.8	5	3.1	97.5
55.00–59.99.....	29	4.5	88.3	3	1.9	99.4
60.00–64.99.....	16	2.5	90.8	1	0.6	100.0
65.00–69.99.....	19	3.0	93.8	—	—	—
70.00–74.99.....	11	1.7	95.5	—	—	—
75.00 and over...	29	4.5	100.0	—	—	—

roll, the number of Negro men was large in the following departments and classifications of employment: cutting floor, lithographers, janitors, loading gang, roustabouts, the lard pail division of the tin shop, and label room. There were six horse-drivers and six hotel and restaurant workers, two of whom were Negroes. The skilled mechanics, watchmen, automobile-drivers, kitchen and canned dried beef department workers, and clerks in the retail store operated in connection with the plant were white. With one exception the company was silent as to a reason for the distribution. A retail butcher, through his refusal to accept a delivery of meat, is responsible for the debarment of Negro men from positions as delivery truck helpers.

In the stockyards the standard rate for all common and unskilled labor is under 45 cents an hour, while the semi-skilled laborers receive between 45 and 50 cents an hour, and the skilled, over 50 cents. According to this classification, 68.6 per cent of the Negro and 38.6 per cent of the white men were common laborers. Of the white men, 30.5 per cent were semi-skilled workers and of the Negroes 25.8 per cent, bringing the percentage of those receiving under 50 cents an hour to 69.1 and 94.4, respectively. One-fourth (25.9 per cent) of the men were thus placed in the category of skilled workmen, 4.3 per cent of whom were Negroes. Nine (5.6 per cent) of the Negroes were receiving 50 cents and over an hour. The hourly rate of wages of the men employees is shown in Chart VIII.

The 40-hour guarantee of employment is in operation in this plant,[1] but seldom, even during the slack season, does employment run so low. In case it were so reduced, an adjustment would usually be made by working an 8-hour day for 5 days and closing the plant on Saturday. For over 10 hours in any one day, or over 55 hours in any one week, a time and a half rate of wages is the rule. Double time is paid for Sundays and six holidays—Christmas, New Year's Day, Decoration Day, July 4, Labor Day, and Thanksgiving.

The hours worked by the men of the two racial groups are shown in Chart IX and are a reflection of the type of labor each performs. Although the Negro men were work-

[1] See p. 82.

CHART IX

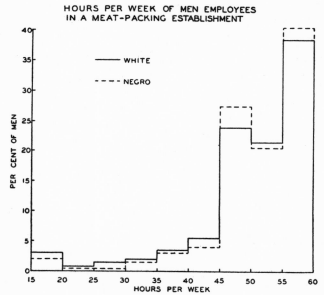

HOURS PER WEEK OF MEN EMPLOYEES
IN A MEAT-PACKING ESTABLISHMENT

NUMBER AND PER CENT DISTRIBUTION AND CUMULATIVE PERCENTAGES

HOURS PER WEEK	WHITE			NEGRO		
	Number	Per cent Distribution	Cumulative Percentage	Number	Per cent Distribution	Cumulative Percentage
Total	743	100.0		170	100.0	
Under 20	24	3.2	3.2	3	1.8	1.8
20 and under 25	6	0.8	4.0	1	0.6	2.4
25 and under 30	9	1.2	5.2	1	0.6	3.0
30 and under 35	11	1.5	6.7	2	1.2	4.2
35 and under 40	27	3.6	10.3	5	2.9	7.1
40 and under 45	40	5.4	15.7	7	4.1	11.2
45 and under 50	181	24.4	40.1	47	27.6	38.8
50 and under 55	159	21.4	61.5	35	20.6	59.4
55 and over	286	38.5	100.0	69	40.6	100.0

ing slightly longer hours than the white, the inference must not be drawn that there is a difference in the daily or weekly hours of white and Negro men performing the same tasks. The explanation lies in the fact that more Negro men occupy the positions which require additional time, such as cleaning up after the day's work, the assembling of finished products, the roustabout and gang work.

At the conclusion of the week (June 12, 1926), the white and Negro men received different amounts of pay, but the difference seems slight when the dissimilarity in their rate of wages is recalled. The additional hours of work which were the Negroes' lot seem scarcely sufficient to produce an equalization in earnings. The weekly earnings of the men are shown in Chart X. Four hundred fifty-five (61.2 per cent) of the white men, and 115 (67.6 per cent) of the Negro men were receiving less than $30 a week. Chart X reveals that the percentage of white men in each succeeding wage group slightly exceeded that of Negro. Five Negroes earned from $40 to $44.99 a week, the highest wage received by a Negro; 31 white men earned a similar amount and 22 more exceeded it.

As in the majority of the leading slaughtering and meat-packing establishments, an incentive plan of wage payment is used. The weekly earnings of laborers are affected by the fact that in this establishment the Bedoux Point System of wage payment is in operation. Under weekly earnings is understood total earnings, the weekly standard rate of wages multiplied by the number of hours worked, to which has been added the premium, if one was received, for production in excess of the 'standard.'

The installation of the Bedoux Wage System has almost eliminated the piece-work system of wage payment.[1] The incentive system incorporates the outstanding feature of the latter system, remuneration based upon production, and has striven to eliminate many of its abuses. Scientific time studies have established the unit of work, a 'B'—the amount of work performed in one minute by a normally

---

[1] In this industry the chief advantage of the hourly system of wage payment is realized at the time of the seasonal interdepartmental transfer of workers.

CHART X

WEEKLY EARNINGS OF MEN EMPLOYEES
IN A MEAT-PACKING ESTABLISHMENT

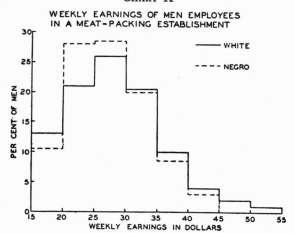

NUMBER AND PER CENT DISTRIBUTION AND CUMULATIVE PERCENTAGES

WEEKLY EARNINGS	WHITE			NEGRO		
	Number	Per cent Distribution	Cumulative Percentage	Number	Per cent Distribution	Cumulative Percentage
Total.........	743	100.0		170	100.0	
Under $20.00....	98	13.2	13.2	18	10.6	10.6
$20.00–$24.99...	165	22.2	35.4	48	28.2	38.8
25.00– 29.99...	192	25.8	61.2	49	28.8	67.6
30.00– 34.99...	160	21.5	82.7	35	20.6	88.2
35.00– 39.99...	75	10.1	92.8	15	8.8	97.0
40.00– 44.99...	31	4.2	97.0	5	3.0	100.0
45.00– 49.99...	15	2.0	99.0	—	—	—
50.00 and over..	7	1.0	100.0	—	—	—

skilled operator working under normal conditions at his normal rate of speed.'[1]   In it are incorporated a fraction of a minute of work plus a fraction of a minute of rest, the aggregate of which is always a minute, but the proportions of which vary according to the operation.   A 'B' value is assigned to each job, with sixty 'B's' established as the normal amount of work per hour.   If production during eight hours exceeds 480 'B's,' a premium has been earned, three-fourths of which goes to the employee, one-fourth to the company, which in turn shares its gain by paying a bonus to the foreman.   This is the foreman's incentive to eliminate all delays and to 'keep things moving.'   Obviously, the system's chief objective is to bring production up to the standard, the sixty 'B's.'   Until this is accomplished, each advance toward it registers a gain for the company; only after the sixty 'B' standard of production has been achieved does the worker benefit by the premium.[2]

Since the basis of the Bedoux Wage System is that of a standard production, the premium earned is an indication of the worker's productive capacity, with the qualifications which will later be enumerated.   When questioned, the workers invariably showed indifference toward the system. Many, judging by their remarks, are utterly unfamiliar with it in spite of the fact that every morning the standard sheet which states the amount of premium earned by each is posted in the various departments.   All they know is that they usually receive two pay checks, one of which is their premium, provided the sum earned is more than a dollar for the week.   The company explains the system of using the two pay checks on the basis of added encouragement given the workers to increase their premiums, but is not unaware of the fact that should it be deemed necessary or advisable to discontinue the system, this method of payment would facilitate matters.   But the premium, according to the workers, seems to rain upon them as a gift from the

---

[1] Arthur H. Carver, *Personnel and Labor Problems in the Packing Industry* (Chicago: The University of Chicago Press, 1928), pp. 128-30.

[2] At the time of the installation of the system, production averaged from 40 to 50 'B's' per hour.   The saving realized by the company, chiefly through the elimination of delays, is almost matched in amount by the sums paid in premiums.

gods. It comes when they are discouraged, when they feel that their wages are not high enough, when they are 'mad' at the foreman or at their team mates. It does not incite envy or emulation, for each sees the system in terms of an opportunity which seldom comes to him, and when it does, he is unable to explain how or why. Since production is generally measured by groups, because of the enormous bookkeeping expense which the system necessitates, the receipt of the premium is not an infallible gauge of the worker's individual productive capacity, even if the system itself were perfect. A further difficulty arises from the fact that the personnel of many gangs and benches is made up of men and women of the two races. On the other hand, work by units or gangs permits of few incompetents. The following groupings according to which premiums are computed will indicate the situation and the difficulties in this type of measurement.

Nine operators compose the fore-quarter cutting line, whose standard production per hour is 334 fore-quarters or 167 cattle. One man 'lugs beef to convey,' a second 'holds the hangers,' a third 'cuts out the foreleg,' two men 'pull the clod and pull away the foreleg,' the sixth man 'shoves it to the saw,' the seventh 'saws the plate,' after which the eighth man on the line 'saws the chuck and rib,' and the ninth saws another portion of the chuck and rib. Nine operators also compose a hind-quarter cutting line, their standard production set at the same mark as for the fore-quarter. The roustabout gang in the beef-cutting department has ten operators. A man is assigned to each of the following tasks: 'fix pulley and wipe hooks,' 'hold hooks,' 'pass beef from car door,' 'put beef on and tend hoist.' Two of the remaining six members of the gang of ten are occupied as 'pushers of beef' (two car lengths), and four 'lug beef from car' (one car length).

The sausage department units are made up of one man who is the 'stuffer', and two or three women who 'link' or 'tie' and 'hang.' In the tin can department most of the units consist of four or five operators. The standard production for soldering tops and bottoms to a pail of given specifications was set at 125 pails per hour. Three of the operators were women. Their tasks were described as 'getting and putting in flux,' 'wiping,' and 'wiping and stacking.' A man 'rolled the pail in the solder.'

A final illustration will be drawn from the round can kitchen in which eighteen operators stuff and can oxford sausage. The standard production is 1,710 cans per hour. One woman 'puts up cans,' four women 'cut links,' two women 'pour first grease' and 'put up links,' four women 'stuff in cans—four links,' three women 'cover with grease and put in cleat,' one woman 'feeds the capper.' Three men complete this unit; one 'operates the capper,' the second, 'inspects,' and the third is the 'batcher.'

Since March, 1923, special time studies have been going on in order gradually to install the system and to correct and perfect it. In spite of the many difficulties involved, the system has been introduced quite generally in the establishment. Changes made in standards, accompanied always by changes in the process, have at times seemed to increase, at others to decrease the amount of premiums workers can earn. The positions held by men not under the Bedoux System are those of the mechanic, both skilled and unskilled, janitors, watchmen, automobile-drivers, loading gang, horse-drivers, and salesmen.

Experts in charge of the Bedoux System maintain that each employee is as capable of obtaining the premium as any other. They unhesitatingly assert that the system not only measures the productive capacity of the worker, but also increases the production of the entire plant. The investigator, however, from the foregoing presentation of the plan, finds insufficient proof that individual production is always so measured. Receipt of the premium can be used as a measure of the worker's productive capacity only by qualifying it by the limitations noted.

Table XII is constructed from the premium amounts received as recorded on the payroll as of the week of June 12, from which the other wage figures were taken. One hundred and two (20.3 per cent) of those in a position to earn a premium failed to do so. All Negro men in a position to earn a premium secured one. Fifty-five of the Negro men were working on tasks not operating under the Bedoux

TABLE XII. EARNINGS OF WHITE AND NEGRO MEN EMPLOYEES AS AFFECTED BY THE BEDOUX PREMIUM SYSTEM OF WAGE PAYMENT

WEEKLY PREMIUMS	TOTAL	WHITE	NEGRO
Total...................	617ᵃ	502	115
No premiums.............	102	102	—
Under $2.50..............	279	230	49
$2.50-$4.99..............	141	111	30
5.00-7.49...............	47	31	16
7.50-9.99...............	32	20	12
10.00 and over...........	16	8	8

ᵃ This figure does not include 296 employees (241 white and 55 negro men) ineligible for premiums.

System; and the same number were receiving no premium. Of those in position to earn a premium, 45.8 per cent of the white men, and 42.6 per cent of the Negro, earned less than $2.50; 22.1 per cent of the former group and 26.1 per cent of the latter earned premiums which ranged from $2.50 to $5.

Occupational Distribution, Rate of Wages, Hours of Employment, Weekly Earnings, and Premiums of Women Employees

Scattered throughout the same plant in some seven or eight departments, 241 white and 123 Negro women were on the payroll at the time of the investigation.

No one set of factors is wholly responsible for the control which is exercised over the numbers and occupations of the colored women. The investigator was informed that Negro women were ineligible for jobs in only one division of the canning department. Some years ago, shortly after the World War, a group of women went through the department in which corned beef was packed. The pressure necessary to force it into the cans causes the fat to run over the girls' hands. The visitors complained against the performance of this operation by Negroes, and since that time none has worked in the department. On the other hand, Negroes are working on the packing of chipped beef.

Visitors pass through this department daily. Small sticks are used as an aid in placing the beef in the jars and apparently no complaints are heard. The jars are lined with the larger pieces. Smaller pieces are folded and pressed into the center, and the ends folded over them. The Negro women for this department are carefully chosen. All employees are dressed in white aprons and caps, and the department is very attractive. There is only one slight manifestation of segregation—the work bench nearest the visitors' route is generally occupied by white girls. In the same room, chipped beef is weighed, and after being packed, is sent to the capping and labeling machines which are operated by Negro and white workmen.

Many women were working in the tin shop. In the dried beef department and in the tin shop proper and in its lard pail division, the number of white and Negro women stood at about the same figure. Thus the number of white women was low in terms of the general ratio of white to Negro women employees. In the round can division of the tin shop, the number of white women was very high, even relatively to the respective sizes of the two groups in the sausage department, the lithographing, and label rooms. According to this classification, no Negro women were working at miscellaneous jobs or in the boullion cube room, and no white women were reported in the square can department.

The hourly rates of wages at which the women were employed (Chart XI) ranged below the level of wages paid to unskilled men. Eighty-five (69.1 per cent) of the Negro women were working at a rate of wages less than $32\frac{1}{2}$ cents an hour, as contrasted with 121 (50.2 per cent) white women employees. Two hundred and four (84.6 per cent) of the white women and 118 (95.9 per cent) of the Negro received less than 35 cents an hour. Few women of either group received more than this amount, the white women having a slight advantage over the colored. The length of the women's working-week is shown in Chart XII. As in the case of the men, the weekly earnings (Chart XIII) of the women include the premiums which were received by a large number. All the Negro women earned less than $25 a week; 19 white women equaled or exceeded that fig-

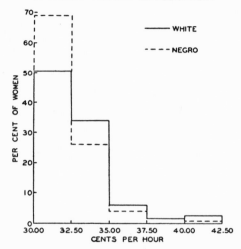

Chart XI

HOURLY RATE OF WAGES OF WOMEN EMPLOYEES
IN A MEAT-PACKING ESTABLISHMENT

NUMBER AND PER CENT DISTRIBUTION AND CUMULATIVE PERCENTAGES

CENTS PER HOUR	WHITE			NEGRO		
	Number	Per cent Distribution	Cumulative Percentage	Number	Per cent Distribution	Cumulative Percentage
Total..........	241	100.0		123	100.0	
30.00–32.49.....	121	50.2	50.2	85	69.1	69.1
32.50–34.99.....	83	34.4	84.6	33	26.8	95.9
35.00–37.49.....	14	5.8	90.4	4	3.3	99.2
37.50–39.99.....	3	1.3	91.7	—	—	99.2
40.00–42.49.....	7	2.9	94.6	1	0.8	100.0
Not reported....	13	5.4	100.0	—	—	—

CHART XII

HOURS PER WEEK OF WOMEN EMPLOYEES
IN A MEAT - PACKING ESTABLISHMENT

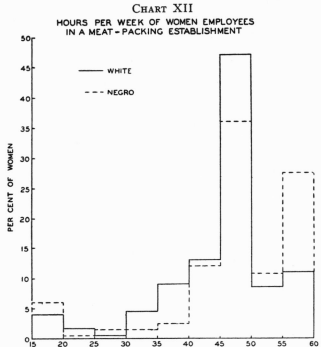

NUMBER AND PER CENT DISTRIBUTION AND CUMULATIVE PERCENTAGES

HOURS PER WEEK	WHITE			NEGRO		
	Number	Per cent Distribution	Cumulative Percentage	Number	Per cent Distribution	Cumulative Percentage
Total....................	241	100.0		123	100.0	
Under 20.................	10	4.1	4.1	8	6.5	6.5
20 and under 25...........	4	1.7	5.8	1	0.8	7.3
25 and under 30...........	2	0.8	6.6	2	1.6	8.9
30 and under 35...........	11	4.6	11.2	2	1.6	10.5
35 and under 40...........	22	9.1	20.3	3	2.4	12.9
40 and under 45...........	32	13.3	33.6	15	12.2	25.1
45 and under 50...........	112	46.5	80.1	44	35.8	60.9
50 and under 55...........	20	8.3	88.4	14	11.4	72.3
55 and over...............	28	11.6	100.0	34	27.7	100.0

CHART XIII

WEEKLY EARNINGS OF WOMEN EMPLOYEES
IN A MEAT-PACKING ESTABLISHMENT

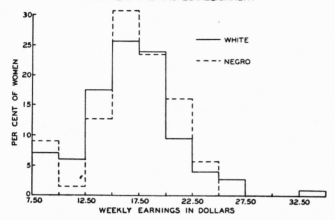

NUMBER AND PER CENT DISTRIBUTION AND CUMULATIVE PERCENTAGES

WEEKLY EARNINGS	WHITE			NEGRO		
	Number	Per cent Distribution	Cumulative Percentage	Number	Per cent Distribution	Cumulative Percentage
Total.........	241	100.0		123	100.0	
Under $10.00....	17	7.1	7.1	11	8.9	8.9
$10.00–$12.49....	15	6.2	13.3	2	1.6	10.5
12.50– 14.99....	44	18.3	31.6	16	13.0	23.5
15.00– 17.49...	63	26.1	57.7	38	30.9	54.4
17.50– 19.99...	58	24.1	81.8	29	23.6	78.0
20.00– 22.49...	23	9.5	91.3	20	16.3	94.3
22.50– 24.99...	10	4.2	95.5	7	5.7	100.0
25.00– 27.49...	7	2.9	98.4	—	—	—
27.50– 29.99...	—	—	—	—	—	—
30.00– 32.49...	—	—	—	—	—	—
32.50– 34.99....	2	0.8	99.2	—	—	—
Not reported...	2	0.8	100.0	—	—	—

ure. The weekly earnings of the Negro women, when
compared with those of the white, appear good. Their
weekly working-hours were longer, and their rates of wages
slightly lower. With an equal opportunity to earn premiums, after five and one-half days of labor their pay checks
were almost the same. That is, the Negro women were
better premium earners than the white, as shown in Table
XIII. Only 2 white women in the entire establishment

TABLE XIII. EARNINGS OF WHITE AND NEGRO WOMEN EMPLOYEES
AS AFFECTED BY THE BEDOUX PREMIUM SYSTEM OF WAGE
PAYMENT

WEEKLY PREMIUMS	TOTAL	WHITE	NEGRO
Total..................	362[a]	239	123
No premium..............	44	36	8
Under $2.50.	196	130	66
$2.50–$4.99	81	52	29
5.00–7.49	37	18	19
7.50–9.99	2	1	1
10.00 and over...........	2	2	—

[a] This figure does not include 2 white women employees ineligible for premiums.

were working on tasks which were outside the Bedoux System. Of the number eligible, 36 white women and 8 Negro
women did not earn premiums, these being 15.1 and 6.5 per
cent of the two groups, respectively. Of those receiving
less than $2.50, and $2.50 but under $5, the percentages of
the total for white and Negro women stood at about the
same figure. Twenty-one (8.8 per cent) white women and
20 (16.3 per cent) Negro earned premiums of $5 or more.

*Yearly and Average Weekly Earnings of Men and Women
Employees from 1922 to 1926*

Each test which suggests itself as a measure of the productive capacity or efficiency of individual workmen presents some degree of unreliability, and, when applied to
two racial groups for purposes of comparison, is invariably
open to additional inaccuracies, if not fallacies. A controlled

experiment could be attempted if individuals, differing only in skin pigmentation, could be found equally well trained and qualified for a given industrial process, performing the same operation at the same rates of pay. This method was applied to a small sample. Yearly earnings were taken as the measure of the worker's productive capacity. In order to do this, men and women of similar ages who had worked steadily throughout the year, with little loss of time, were chosen. For at least one year they had all been working on jobs which required no special degree of skill. With these qualifications the selections were made at random.

Little variation was found between the yearly earnings of 5 white and 5 Negro men employed on the loading gang or those of 6 men of each racial group in the cutting department. In each case, the earnings of the white men were slightly higher than those of the Negro. The women reversed the situation. Study was made of the yearly earnings of 4 white and 4 Negro women employed in the tin shop at 30 cents an hour, operating the same machine, and of 2 white and 2 Negro women working under similar circumstances, at the hourly rate of 33 cents. The yearly earnings of the Negro were a little higher than those of the white women. The cases are too few from which to draw conclusions, but are of interest as a sample of the relative earning powers of the two groups. In 1926, the average weekly earnings of men and women, as compiled from payrolls, show a slight increase over the earnings of the previous three years, being $29.99 and $21.59, respectively, for men, and $17.62 and $13.31, respectively, for women.

While work assignments are insufficient in themselves to show that the company adhered to a labor policy affected by racial preference, confirmatory evidence is provided by a study of the *Labor Analysis* records and the weekly payroll. Nevertheless, proof of this fact is difficult to establish. Wage-earners of the two groups are found working together; in gangs employed as a unit, the highest paid position is sometimes held by a Negro, sometimes by a white worker; there is no well-defined scheme for assigning positions to workers of the one race to the exclusion of those of the other. And for this very reason, an analysis of the wage-rates received by the Negro and white workers and their weekly hours makes the covert preference even more subtle and significant. Moreover, the earning capacity of the colored group as demonstrated by weekly earnings and the premiums, although far from conclusive, rules out the assumption of their lack of ability and industrial efficiency as the only explanation of their status and rates of pay.

CHAPTER VII

COMPARATIVE LABOR MOBILITY OF WHITE AND NEGRO EMPLOYEES

THE eventual as well as the present position of the Negro in industry is sooner or later treated in the light of his real or supposed unreliability. Whatever his productive capacity, his sense of 'loyalty,' his accident or sickness rate, unless he can be counted upon to appear on the job from day to day, his employment is costly to the employer. Employers unanimously complain of his unsteadiness, of the rapid rate at which he passes through establishments in the yards, of his casualness in 'throwing up a job.' In interviewing those connected with numerous establishments in the same industry, identical phrases are not infrequently heard to describe the situation as well as to interpret it: twice as many Negroes as one wishes to use must be kept on the payroll; they do not seem to want to stay; they have 'no sense about a job'; they lay off on account of minor ailments, domestic difficulties, marital troubles, and lawsuits.

A rate of 'labor turnover' is readily secured from the employment secretaries or managers of even the smaller stockyard firms. In some instances this is given as one figure for males and another for females, but an accurate turnover rate by race and sex cannot be secured. As estimates of labor mobility are in most cases obtained by the process of a simple division of total separations from service by total number of employees, ambiguities exist. This section of the study seeks to employ a dependable method to measure labor fluctuations, and to serve as a reliable mode for comparing the mobility of white and Negro wage-earners.

The high rate of labor mobility—the so-called 'labor turnover' figure—of slaughtering and meat-packing establishments is frequently nothing more or less than a measure of the degree of seasonal fluctuation in the industry, over which the worker has no control, as shown in preceding sections of the study. The average number of wage-earners by months, in the United States and for the State of Illinois, for 1919, 1921, 1923, and 1925 are shown in Table XIV. In Illinois the reduction in the number of wage-earners during the slack season ranged from 23.1 per cent of the maximum number of employees in 1919 to 13.6 per cent in 1925.; for the United States as a whole, from 19.6 per cent of the maximum number of employees in 1919 to 14.2 per cent in 1925. Employment fluctuations within the selected establishment compiled from the *Labor Analysis* revealed an irregularity of employment much greater than the Government statistics indicated for Illinois or for the country as a whole. From 1,000 to 1,300 fewer were employed during the period of idleness in the spring than during the mid-winter period of maximum employment. The high rate of 'turnover' may be characteristic of a small percentage of workers who are as steady as seasonal demand permits. Discharge during slack periods and hiring during the busier seasons should not be considered in measuring the mobility of laborers unaffected by seasonal variations, but should be dealt with in an inclusive way to cover the whole problem of labor mobility. Moreover, workmen are victims of a second set of circumstances which greatly affect their ability to maintain steady employment; namely, the cyclical periods of business depression and expansion, which are less frequent but more violent.[1]

Two aspects of labor mobility are considered; first, the

[1] A few definitions will make it easier to understand the method of measuring labor changes which has been adopted. *Labor mobility* refers to the total labor changes in and out of the establishment. The *accessions* are the number of employees hired, the *separations* are those leaving. The *replacements* are the number of separating workers who are replaced to keep up the work force. *Labor turnover* is the term used to designate the number of replacements necessary to maintain the normal plant force. The normal plant force is the number of 300-day workers to which the total days worked are calculated to be equivalent. The 300-day standard has been arbitrarily adopted as the labor time worked by the average fully employed worker. This employee is designated as the *full-year worker*. The number of full-year workers is obtained by dividing the total number of days worked during the period by 300. All rates of labor change are computed on this base, by dividing labor changes of whatever kind by the number of full-year workers. For example the accession rate is obtained by dividing the number hired for a given period by the number of days worked during the period and multiplying by 300. Or the number of labor changes may be divided by the number of full-year workers. See Paul F. Brissenden and Emil Frankel, *Labor Turnover in Industry* (New York: The Macmillan Company, 1922.)

TABLE XIV. WAGE-EARNERS, BY MONTHS, FOR THE UNITED STATES AND ILLINOIS, 1919 to 1925,[a] SLAUGHTERING AND MEAT-PACKING

	AVERAGE NUMBER EMPLOYED DURING YEAR	NUMBER EMPLOYED ON 15TH DAY OF MONTH OR THE NEAREST REPRESENTATIVE DAY												PER CENT MINIMUM FORMS OF MAXIMUM
		January	February	March	April	May	June	July	August	September	October	November	December	
United States:														
1925[b]	120,422	131,970*	125,822	119,033	113,193	114,710	118,053	118,835	116,957	117,631	119,668	123,688	125,501	85.8
1923[b]	132,792	133,907	127,257	126,432	126,216	126,350	131,919	133,657	134,837	134,361	137,662	139,748	141,163*	89.4
1921[b]	117,042	126,811*	124,399	115,949	107,124	111,243	114,217	116,946	115,744	116,006	117,005	122,691	115,776	84.5
1919[b]	160,996	187,609*	171,452	163,025	150,806	151,252	157,358	157,938	156,304	154,147	155,398	158,859	167,804	80.4
Illinois:														
1925[b]	30,236	32,891*	31,425	29,574	28,410	28,935	29,617	29,818	29,875	30,258	30,235	30,833	30,955	86.4
1923[b]	36,144	34,931	32,919	33,317	33,575	34,813	36,422	37,204	37,504	37,076	38,354	39,158*	38,452	84.1
1921[b]	32,136	35,823*	34,822	31,472	28,820	30,002	30,749	32,033	32,290	32,389	33,390	34,316	29,530	80.5
1919[b]	54,179	65,114*	59,864	55,397	50,447	50,048	51,711	52,297	52,435	52,671	54,946	53,729	53,509	76.9

[a] United States Bureau of the Census, Census of Manufactures: 1925, Slaughtering and Meat-Packing, pp. 7–8; Census of Manufactures: 1923, Slaughtering and Meat-Packing, p. 6; Census of Manufactures: 1921, Slaughtering and Meat-Packing, p. 8; Fourteenth Census of the United States, 1920, IX, p. 316.
[b] Month of maximum employment indicated by asterisk.

number of replacements (separated employees who were replaced) necessary to maintain a normal working force, and second, the flow in and out of the plant, which is perhaps the best single indication of stability. Thus, accessions as well as separations are used in the computation.

The rates of accession and separation per equivalent full-year worker are computed as an index of the amount of shifting involved and the extent of the increase and decrease within the establishment. From these two rates the replacement and flux rates are obtained. The latter is significant in that it gives not only the accessions which are replacements, but the recruits added to the working force who are not replacements, as well as those who leave and are not replaced, and is thus a measure of the total mobility of the labor force.

The analysis of the labor replacement and flux rates of white and Negro employees will be followed by that of the separation rates. By the method of rating used throughout the section, the rate per full-year worker of those resigning, discharged, or laid off will be presented for the four groups of workers. In conclusion, length of service will be commented upon.

Labor Replacement and Flux Rates

Since, for the purpose of this study, labor replacements have been decided upon as the most accurate means of measuring the fluctuations of the labor force involved in its maintenance, and since the standard working force has been made the equivalent of the number of full-year 300-day workers, the rate of the labor flow is the rate of the variable to the base. If the number of replacements is divided by the number of 300-day workers, the result is the rate of replacement for each 300-day worker, or the replacement rate per full-year worker.

Table XV shows that the replacement rate for the white men was lower than that for the other three groups of workers for three of the four years covered. In 1923-24, the replacement rate for Negro men and women was lower than that for white. With this one exception in the case of Negro women the replacement rate for women was never so low as that for white men; in 1922-23, the replacement rate for white women was lower than that for Negro men; during 1922-23 and 1925-26, the replacement rate for Negro women was lower than that for Negro men. The white and Negro men show a similarity and a comparability in replacement rates which is also true of the women when classified according to race. The rate of replacement was higher for white women than for Negro during three years covered by the study; in 1922-23, the rate for Negro women was higher than for white.

The labor flux rates of the total employees, by race and sex, for the period from December 2, 1922, to November 27, 1926, inclusive, is shown in Table XVI. An ab-

TABLE XV. LABOR REPLACEMENT RATES OF EMPLOYEES BY RACE AND SEX, DECEMBER 2, 1922, TO NOVEMBER 27, 1926, INCLUSIVE

YEARa	MEN		WOMEN	
	White	Negro	White	Negro
1922–1923...........	.121	.269	.158	.257
1923–1924...........	.107	.097	.119	.101
1924–1925...........	.096	.100	.136	.121
1925–1926...........	.092	.122	.135	.117

a The twelve-month period in each case is from December to November of the following year, inclusive.

TABLE XVI. LABOR FLUX RATES OF EMPLOYEES BY RACE AND SEX, DECEMBER 2, 1922, TO NOVEMBER 27, 1926, INCLUSIVE

YEARa	MEN		WOMEN	
	White	Negro	White	Negro
1922–1923...........	.332	.699	.455	.706
1923–1924...........	.270	.280	.353	.334
1924–1925...........	.259	.271	.379	.355
1925–1926...........	.265	.353	.409	.422

a The twelve-month period in each case is from December to November of the following year, inclusive.

normal instability of all wage-earners for the year 1922-23 was more applicable to the Negro workers than to the white, and the Negro women showed greater fluctuation in employment than the Negro men. For the four years, the rate per full-year worker for white men was very much lower than that for any other group of workers; in fact, the flux rates of the two women's groups never sank to the point which constituted the highest rate for the white men for the same period. Extremes were less marked in the flux rate of the white men than in those of the other groups. In the case of the Negro men, the high rate of the first recorded year appeared so extreme that it seemed entirely disparate from the rate for the other years. A great improvement was noted in the drop of the rate for the following two years, and even in the rise of 1925-26. The improvement in the flux rate of the two groups of women was somewhat more pronounced for the Negro than for the white. In 1925-26, an increase occurred in the flux rate of all workers, the rate being highest for the Negro women.

The mobility rates from year to year showing a composite picture of labor changes did not reflect the striking differences occurring from month to month. These differences existed between the monthly and yearly accession and separation rates and corresponding flux rates of each group of workers (white and Negro men and women). Furthermore, the figures representing the monthly trend of labor changes of each group of workers, considered separately, presented striking variations. The marked dissimilarities in either case were due to seasonality, labor policy, and the general conditions of industrial activity.

The yearly flux rates cover a wide range of mobility. In 1922-23, the relatively high flux rates were a result of the period of business expansion. The entire labor force was augmented; accessions were in excess of separations from nine to eleven months of the year for the different groups. But the extremes in variation were much greater for the Negro than for the white workers. February, 1923, a low flux rate of .258 was recorded for the Negro men; in June, the rate stood at 1.119. The colored women showed a range in flux rates from .288 in May to 1.033 in January.

The business depression of 1924 caused all flux rates to fall. The variations in labor changes of the white men corresponded with the seasonal demands of employment. In the summer of 1924, during the slack season, the low flux rate (.104) showed the greatest stability of employment reached during the four-year period; in September, October, and November, as the establishment increased the number of employees, the highest flux rate (.479) was recorded. The striking decrease in the flux rate of the Negro men in 1923-24 is readily explicable from the fact that during eight months separations were in excess of accessions; the number of Negro men was reduced faster than that of any other group. The flux rates of the two groups of women also decreased during the depression of 1924. Greater stability is noted in the case of white women despite the increase in the actual number of white women hired from August to November, 1924. The Negro women cut the flux rate of the preceding year in half. A marked decrease was recorded in both the accession and separation rates, and in the actual number of colored women who passed in and out of the establishment.

In 1924-25 and 1925-26, the period of greatest stability (lowest flux) again occurred during the late winter and early spring; the flux rate rose during the late fall and early winter with greater variation occurring in the high and low flux rates of women than in those of men. The greatest mobility was recorded for the Negro women whose flux rates varied in 1925 from .132 in February to .924 in August, and in 1926 from .082 in April to .871 in September.

Rate of Separation and Length of Service

The relative stability of white and Negro workmen may be viewed in the light of another set of figures, those obtained from a consideration of the reasons for leaving the establishment. In terms of the classification given in the *Labor Analysis,* they occur as 'left voluntarily,' 'discharged,' and 'laid off.' The lay-offs represent changes which are a result of a scarcity of work. In Tables XVII, XVIII, XIX, and XX are given the number and rate per full-year worker of employees (by race and sex) leaving voluntarily, discharged, and laid off, from December 2, 1922, to November 27, 1926, inclusive. A summary of the data for each year appears in Tables XXI, XXII, and XXIII.

The rate per full-year worker of separations, classified according to reason for terminating the employment, is not divided equally among the working force. The most distinctive differences will be noted: first, the dissimilarity in the chief cause of separations of colored and white wage-earners; and second, the difference in the *rates* per full-year worker of voluntary leaving, discharge, and lay-off of members of the two racial groups.

For the four-year period, voluntary leaving was the chief cause of the separations of the white men and women. This was also true for the Negro men during the first and last years covered by the study, and for the Negro women for the first and third years. In 1924-25, the rate per full-year worker of Negro men who left voluntarily was the same as the rate for those laid off. During approximately half the period, most separations of Negro men and women were due to slackness of work. Discharges were never an outstanding cause; the rate of discharge was more stable, less subject to variation than the rate of lay-off and voluntary leaving.

Second, the *rates* at which workers left the establishment, voluntarily or otherwise, were different for each race and sex group. Excluding the year 1922-23, the rate per full-year worker of those who left voluntarily was higher for white men than for Negro, and for white women than for Negro. The two extremes in high and low rates of quitting were those of white women and Negro men, respectively; the rates for white men and Negro women standing midway between the two. For the four-year period, the greatest reduction in the rate at which workers quit occurred in the case of Negro men, followed by that of Negro women and white men; the rate of white women was practically stationary. The lay-off rate of all workers increased during the period and was much higher for Negro men and women than for white; the rate at which Negro women were laid off exceeded that of Negro men. The discharge rate per

TABLE XVII. TYPE OF SEPARATION (DISCHARGE, LAY-OFF, OR VOLUNTARY QUITTING) OF WHITE MEN BY MONTHS, FROM DECEMBER, 1922, TO NOVEMBER, 1926, INCLUSIVE

YEAR AND MONTH	NUMBER				RATE PER FULL-YEAR WORKER			
	Total	Voluntary Separations	Discharges	Lay-Offs	Total	Voluntary Separation	Discharge	Lay-Off
1922								
December..	182	134	47	1	.122	.090	.031	.001
1923								
January....	171	105	43	23	.143	.088	.036	.019
February...	147	103	17	27	.125	.088	.014	.023
March.....	266ᵃ	147	25	50	.194	.107	.018	.036
April......	134	110	24	..	.141	.116	.025	.000
May.......	68	62	4	2	.141	.129	.008	.004
June.......	127	112	14	1	.091	.080	.010	.001
July.......	85	65	17	3	.089	.068	.018	.003
August.....	97	78	19	..	.099	.080	.019	.000
September..	153	107	44	2	.114	.080	.033	.001
October....	153	110	41	2	.130	.093	.035	.002
November..	153	90	42	21	.118	.070	.032	.016
December..	204	116	64	24	.126	.072	.039	.015
1924								
January....	186	47	16	123	.158	.040	.014	.104
February...	89	29	13	47	.084	.027	.012	.045
March.....	118	62	14	42	.096	.051	.011	.034
April......	118	87	16	15	.119	.088	.016	.015
May.......	110	65	10	35	.094	.056	.008	.030
June.......	63	38	5	20	.072	.043	.006	.023
July.......	42	29	8	5	.049	.034	.009	.006
August.....	78	48	29	1	.069	.042	.026	.001
September..	182	130	49	3	.165	.118	.044	.003
October....	229	172	50	7	.187	.140	.041	.006
November..	316	219	78	19	.194	.134	.048	.012
December..	184	136	47	1	.144	.106	.037	.001
1925								
January....	257	121	32	104	.180	.085	.022	.073
February...	92	41	18	33	.119	.053	.023	.043
March.....	173	45	9	119	.176	.046	.009	.121
April......	104	53	18	33	.117	.060	.020	.037
May.......	81	59	13	9	.075	.055	.012	.008
June.......	55	33	12	10	.065	.039	.014	.012
July.......	54	33	11	10	.062	.038	.013	.011
August.....	143	110	30	3	.119	.092	.025	.002
September..	171	121	29	21	.170	.120	.029	.021
October....	155	103	38	14	.113	.075	.028	.010
November..	226	164	44	18	.185	.134	.036	.015
December..	192	100	13	79	.171	.089	.012	.070
1926								
January....	229	68	10	151	.182	.054	.008	.120
February...	80	44	9	27	.085	.047	.009	.029
March.....	83	48	4	31	.096	.055	.005	.036
April......	93	60	8	25	.111	.072	.009	.030
May.......	148	60	6	82	.156	.063	.006	.087
June.......	84	68	14	2	.099	.080	.017	.002
July.......	92	76	16	..	.084	.069	.015	.000
August.....	147	118	15	14	.153	.122	.016	.015
September..	119	91	24	4	.117	.090	.023	.004
October....	145	115	30	..	.123	.097	.026	.000
November..	260	194	41	25	.172	.128	.027	.017
December..	..	..	..	..	..	..	..	..

ᵃ Total includes 44 transferred.

TABLE XVIII. TYPE OF SEPARATION (DISCHARGE, LAY-OFF, OR VOLUNTARY QUITTING) OF NEGRO MEN BY MONTHS, FROM DECEMBER, 1922, TO NOVEMBER, 1926, INCLUSIVE

YEAR AND MONTH	NUMBER				RATE PER FULL-YEAR WORKER			
	Total	Voluntary Separations	Discharges	Lay-Offs	Total	Voluntary Separation	Discharge	Lay-Off
1922								
December..	184	86	70	28	.397	.186	.151	.060
1923								
January....	104	29	18	57	.368	.103	.064	.201
February...	31	14	6	11	.129	.058	.025	.046
March.....	69ᵃ	31	27	7	.226	.101	.088	.023
April......	71	45	25	1	.309	.196	.109	.004
May.......	45	30	9	6	.391	.261	.078	.052
June.......	152	94	56	2	.404	.250	.149	.005
July.......	99	49	46	4	.290	.143	.135	.012
August.....	107	58	48	1	.285	.154	.128	.003
September..	132	49	74	9	.244	.090	.137	.017
October....	101	55	43	3	.212	.116	.090	.006
November..	98	30	32	36	.216	.066	.071	.079
December..	109	40	25	44	.217	.080	.050	.087
1924								
January....	86	11	2	73	.295	.038	.007	.250
February...	39	9	9	21	.147	.034	.034	.079
March.....	44	9	6	29	.141	.029	.019	.093
April......	21	8	9	4	.087	.033	.037	.017
May.......	48	15	11	22	.176	.055	.040	.081
June.......	18	9	..	9	.094	.047	.000	.047
July.......	11	5	4	2	.060	.027	.022	.011
August.....	12	4	8	..	.043	.014	.029	.000
September..	56	32	20	4	.269	.154	.096	.019
October....	32	19	12	1	.124	.074	.046	.004
November..	62ᵇ	24	17	14	.176	.068	.048	.040
December..	43	22	11	10	.167	.085	.043	.039
1925								
January....	55	8	8	39	.186	.027	.027	.132
February...	16	3	2	11	.097	.018	.012	.067
March.....	26	6	2	18	.138	.032	.010	.096
April......	24	8	3	13	.139	.046	.018	.075
May.......	24	7	2	15	.118	.034	.010	.074
June.......	13	11	1	1	.080	.068	.006	.006
July.......	10	3	6	1	.058	.017	.035	.006
August.....	23	12	11	..	.095	.050	.045	.000
September..	34	21	11	2	.157	.097	.051	.009
October....	61	19	17	25	.193	.060	.054	.079
November..	44	24	9	11	.153	.084	.031	.038
December..	55	14	13	28	.205	.052	.049	.104
1926								
January....	88	17	..	71	.311	.060	.000	.251
February...	26	11	1	14	.128	.054	.005	.069
March.....	20	10	4	6	.106	.053	.021	.032
April......	27	7	6	14	.155	.040	.035	.080
May.......	27	9	3	15	.138	.046	.015	.077
June.......	15	12	3	..	.091	.073	.018	.000
July.......	23	12	11	..	.087	.045	.042	.000
August.....	45	28	10	7	.194	.121	.043	.030
September..	50	17	32	1	.193	.066	.123	.004
October....	83	33	38	12	.219	.087	.100	.032
November..	46	25	18	3	.154	.084	.060	.010
December..	..	..	..	..	..	..	..	..

ᵃ Total includes 4 transferred.
ᵇ Data missing for type of separation for one week.

TABLE XIX. TYPE OF SEPARATION (DISCHARGE, LAY-OFF, OR VOLUNTARY QUITTING) OF WHITE WOMEN BY MONTHS, FROM DECEMBER, 1922, TO NOVEMBER, 1926, INCLUSIVE

YEAR AND MONTH	NUMBER				RATE PER FULL-YEAR WORKER			
	Total	Voluntary Separations	Discharges	Lay-Offs	Total	Voluntary Separation	Discharge	Lay-Off
1922								
December..	59	51	4	4	.143	.123	.010	.010
1923								
January....	59	48	2	9	.177	.144	.006	.027
February...	57	52	4	1	.193	.176	.014	.003
March......	121a	69	1	27	.348	.198	.003	.078
April......	28	25	3	..	.092	.082	.010	.000
May.......	21	16	5	..	.145	.110	.035	.000
June.......	45	35	..	10	.128	.100	.000	.028
July.......	40	38	2	..	.137	.130	.007	.000
August.....	28	27	1	..	.085	.082	.003	.000
September..	59	54	1	4	.158	.145	.002	.011
October....	48	42	6	..	.151	.132	.019	.000
November..	61	54	4	3	.173	.153	.011	.009
December..	53	39	1	13	.110	.081	.002	.027
1924								
January....	74	35	2	37	.213	.101	.006	.106
February...	21	16	..	5	.075	.057	.000	.018
March.....	46	26	..	20	.141	.080	.000	.061
April......	24	22	2	..	.100	.092	.008	.000
May.......	51	33	4	14	.168	.109	.013	.046
June.......	14	12	..	2	.058	.050	.000	.008
July.......	16	13	2	1	.067	.054	.009	.004
August.....	55	49	6	..	.143	.127	.016	.000
September..	55	55	..	..	.128	.128	.000	.000
October....	91	89	2	..	.191	.187	.004	.000
November..	158b	110	10	5	.272	.189	.017	.009
December..	98	93	2	3	.219	.208	.004	.007
1925								
January....	88	83	4	1	.180	.170	.008	.002
February...	50	39	11	..	.177	.138	.039	.000
March.....	129	41	4	84	.373	.118	.012	.243
April......	33	26	..	7	.119	.094	.000	.025
May.......	33	26	7	..	.105	.083	.022	.000
June.......	22	19	1	2	.083	.071	.004	.008
July.......	19	19	..	..	.068	.068	.000	.000
August.....	86	78	8	..	.202	.183	.019	.000
September..	100	87	9	4	.250	.218	.022	.010
October....	73	52	2	19	.148	.106	.004	.038
November..	114	101	13	..	.239	.212	.027	.000
December..	112	67	5	40	.251	.150	.011	.090
1926								
January....	126	53	1	72	.300	.126	.002	.172
February...	35	24	..	11	.111	.076	.000	.035
March.....	43	24	2	17	.145	.081	.007	.057
April......	65	24	..	41	.231	.085	.000	.146
May.......	40	10	1	29	.147	.037	.004	.106
June.......	28	26	2	..	.124	.115	.009	.000
July.......	49	43	6	..	.135	.118	.017	.000
August.....	94	77	1	16	.263	.215	.003	.045
September..	85	75	4	6	.249	.220	.012	.017
October....	116	90	24	2	.222	.172	.046	.004
November..	87	65	2	20	.233	.174	.005	.054
December..	..	..	..	..	..	..	..	..

a Total includes 24 transferred.
b Data missing for type of separation for one week.

TABLE XX. TYPE OF SEPARATION (DISCHARGE, LAY-OFF, OR VOLUNTARY QUITTING) OF NEGRO WOMEN BY MONTHS, FROM DECEMBER, 1922, TO NOVEMBER, 1926, INCLUSIVE

YEAR AND MONTH	NUMBER				RATE PER FULL-YEAR WORKER			
	Total	Voluntary Separations	Discharges	Lay-Offs	Total	Voluntary Separation	Discharge	Lay-Off
1922								
December..	134	114	19	1	.392	.333	.056	.003
1923								
January....	78	68	10	..	.321	.280	.041	.000
February...	79	55	14	10	.287	.200	.051	.036
March.....	176ᵃ	69	35	40	.492	.193	.098	.112
April......	77	43	14	20	.363	.203	.066	.094
May.......	15	9	2	4	.188	.113	.025	.050
June.......	54	33	16	5	.202	.123	.060	.019
July.......	45	33	12	..	.193	.142	.051	.000
August.....	45	32	5	8	.190	.135	.021	.034
September..	92	47	33	12	.276	.141	.099	.036
October....	59	25	13	21	.167	.071	.037	.059
November..	121	56	21	44	.337	.156	.058	.123
December..	82	40	14	28	.213	.104	.036	.073
1924								
January....	110	19	7	84	.507	.088	.032	.387
February...	19	7	3	9	.116	.043	.018	.055
March.....	35	9	6	20	.158	.041	.027	.090
April......	13	5	6	2	.077	.030	.035	.012
May.......	26	14	2	10	.129	.069	.010	.050
June.......	25	9	..	16	.205	.074	.000	.131
July.......	6	6	..	..	.052	.052	.000	.000
August.....	22	15	7	..	.107	.073	.034	.000
September..	25	17	2	6	.137	.093	.011	.033
October....	21	15	4	2	.097	.069	.019	.009
November..	42	16	3	23	.194	.074	.014	.106
December..	21	17	2	2	.129	.105	.012	.012
1925								
January....	30	7	2	21	.157	.037	.010	.110
February...	7	4	3	..	.066	.038	.028	.000
March.....	24	6	1	17	.170	.042	.007	.121
April......	21	2	..	19	.191	.018	.000	.173
May.......	14	6	2	6	.100	.043	.014	.043
June.......	25	11	3	11	.209	.092	.025	.092
July.......	16	5	4	7	.150	.047	.037	.066
August.....	41	28	13	..	.238	.163	.075	.000
September..	49	27	11	11	.284	.156	.064	.064
October....	36	15	9	12	.170	.071	.042	.057
November..	41	28	6	7	.143	.098	.021	.024
December..	96	16	3	77	.561	.094	.017	.450
1926								
January....	42	10	1	31	.255	.061	.006	.188
February...	10	4	1	5	.073	.030	.007	.036
March.....	22	7	..	15	.188	.060	.000	.128
April......	8	5	1	2	.073	.046	.009	.018
May.......	15	9	..	6	.117	.070	.000	.047
June.......	16	12	4	..	.126	.094	.032	.000
July.......	29	7	8	14	.153	.037	.042	.074
August.....	29	25	3	1	.157	.136	.016	.005
September..	44	32	11	1	.189	.137	.048	.004
October....	136	70	13	53	.379	.195	.036	.148
November..	70	22	7	41	.286	.090	.029	.167
December..	..	..	..	...	..	..	..	..

ᵃ Total includes 32 transferred.

TABLE XXI. RATE PER FULL-YEAR WORKER OF SEPARATED EMPLOYEES WHO WERE DISCHARGED, BY RACE AND SEX, DECEMBER 2, 1922, TO NOVEMBER 27, 1926, INCLUSIVE

YEAR[a]	MEN		WOMEN	
	White	Negro	White	Negro
1922–1923	.023	.102	.010	.055
1923–1924	.023	.036	.006	.020
1924–1925	.022	.029	.013	.028
1925–1926	.014	.043	.010	.020

[a] The twelve-month period in each case is from December to November of the following year, inclusive.

TABLE XXII. RATE PER FULL-YEAR WORKER OF SEPARATED EMPLOYEES WHO WERE LAID OFF, BY RACE AND SEX, DECEMBER 2, 1922, TO NOVEMBER 27, 1926, INCLUSIVE

YEAR[a]	MEN		WOMEN	
	White	Negro	White	Negro
1922–1923	.009	.042	.014	.047
1923–1924	.025	.061	.023	.079
1924–1925	.030	.052	.028	.064
1925–1926	.034	.057	.061	.105

[a] The twelve-month period in each case is from December to November of the following year, inclusive.

TABLE XXIII. RATE PER FULL-YEAR WORKER OF SEPARATED EMPLOYEES WHO LEFT VOLUNTARILY, BY RACE AND SEX, DECEMBER 2, 1922 TO NOVEMBER 27, 1926, INCLUSIVE

YEAR[a]	MEN		WOMEN	
	White	Negro	White	Negro
1922–1923	.091	.144	.131	.174
1923–1924	.070	.054	.105	.068
1924–1925	.075	.052	.139	.076
1925–1926	.081	.065	.131	.088

[a] The twelve-month period in each case is from December to November of the following year, inclusive.

full-year worker for the four years was higher for Negro men than for any other group of workers. It was followed by that for Negro women, white men, and white women, respectively, except during 1923-24, when the rate for Negro women was lower than that for white men. All classes of workers showed a decrease in their discharge rates; this was especially true for Negro men, and was noticeable for Negro women.

A more minute comparison of the rates per full-year worker of lay-off, resignation, and discharge by race and sex adds little to that already noted. It introduces, however, two facts of relatively minor importance; namely, the frequency of discharge as compared with the rate of separation for other causes, and the range in the rates of separation for the three specified reasons. In 1922-23, the discharge rate per full-year worker was second in importance as a cause of separation for all but the white women; the following three years it ranked third for all workers. The rate at which white men and women quit was greatly in excess of their rates of lay-off and discharge. A comparable difference in the respective rates of the three types of separation did not exist among the Negro workers, despite the lower rate of discharge. In other words, there was less variation in the lay-off and voluntary quitting rates of Negro than in those of white workers.

The rate at which various workers decide to give up their jobs is worthy of special scrutiny. While the discharge rate for Negro men was higher than that for white, and for Negro women than for white, and the lay-off rate was also higher, nevertheless, making due allowance for the year 1922-23, the rate which shows their tendency to stick by a job—the rate of quitting—was considerably lower for Negro men and women than for white. The rate was much the highest for white women, followed by that for Negro women, with the rate for white men being in turn higher than that for Negro men. The rate of quitting by Negroes was much higher in 1923, the year employment was best for all workers and in particular for colored applicants. They took more chances than did white laborers, when the two groups were most nearly comparable in the degree of success with which they could obtain work.

This year of industrial prosperity and heavy Negro migration affords interesting comparisons in the conduct of colored and white workers and warrants further comment. The discharge rate of Negro men was very much higher than that of other workers and continued higher for the following years. The lay-off rate in 1922-23 was much higher for Negro than for white workers, whose rate for the year was very low. In 1923-24, the rate of lay-off of all workers rose, but in particular that of the colored, and the rate at which wage-earners left the establishment for other causes declined. Seeing an opportunity to hire white workers, employers dismissed the colored.

The favorable conditions of employment in 1923, resulting in the high rates of separation and mobility of labor, were reflected in the seasonal employment cycle. Employees did not leave in the summer, when workers were restless, when outdoor employment for common laborers was available, and when the heat increased and intensified the odors and filth of the yards and added to the unpleasantness of the industry. Their highest flux rate occurred during those months when the working force was being augmented, which in some years began as early as September, and in others was not noticeable until October, November, or December. During the last months of the year, both the accession and separation rates reached their maximum. If this were true only in the case of the workers who left because they were discharged, it might be conceded that the incompetency of new workers was responsible. But the resignation rate was highest in September, October, November, and December, the same months in which it was highest for those who were discharged. The exception to this was 1923, the year in which the rate of resignation reached its height in March, April, and May. The Negro employee of recent migration differs in no way from the white man as regards the season of the year in which his separation rate is highest. The attention of wage-earners is closely focused upon the particular situation of which they are a part. It seems to matter but little to them whether the state of the general labor market corresponds with that of the one in which they are immediately concerned. When work is good in meat-packing, they conduct themselves in a way not calculated to establish a low discharge rate, and are apt to take chances in securing other employment, both because of the optimism born of good times and the hope that they may be able to get their old jobs back in the event of failure. Doubtless, too, the rate of turnover among the newest accessions to the force is responsible for many of the separations. When work is slack during the summer months, each worker who has been fortunate enough to keep a job holds on to it.

Separations from the plant, in the words of the employment secretary, occur chiefly among the 'floaters,' certainly among the workers who may be classified as the unskilled. These are the ones who are turned off during reductions in the labor force. In fact the secretary feels that almost the entire labor turnover, for which the seasonality of the industry is largely responsible, is confined to a very small group. The labor force seems a very reliable and stable one to him. For the four years 1922-26, it was found that the length of service of 72.7 per cent of the separations was under three months; 14.7 per cent of the separations worked in the plant from three to six months; of those leaving, only 12.6 per cent had been with the company more than six months.

Tables XXIV, XXV, and XXVI show the length of service of the employees who left voluntarily, were discharged or laid off. There are no records from which it is possible to classify the length of service of the types of separation by sex and race.

For all three types of separation, the greatest percentage left before three months of employment had been completed. For three of the four years the frequency of discharge was more rapid in the service group under three months than that in the other types of separation. It was closely followed by the high frequency rate of separation of those who left voluntarily, and lastly by those laid off. Of those in the service group from three to six months who separated, the highest percentage was laid off; with the exception of the year 1922-23, the same was true for the separation of the workers who had been employed over six months. The percentage of employees discharged was higher for those working less than three months than for those serving three to six months and over six months. To a less degree the same was true of all separations.

The service records of the women employees show least

TABLE XXIV. LENGTH OF SERVICE IN A MEAT-PACKING ESTABLISHMENT OF SEPARATED EMPLOYEES WHO LEFT VOLUNTARILY, DECEMBER 2, 1922, TO NOVEMBER 27, 1926, INCLUSIVE; NUMBER AND PER CENT DISTRIBUTION

YEAR[a]	TOTAL		UNDER 3 MONTHS		3 TO 6 MONTHS		OVER 6 MONTHS	
	Number	Per cent Distribution	Number	Per cent Distribution	Number	Per cent Distribution	Number	Per cent Distribution
1922–1923...	2,888	100.0	2,261	78.3	384	13.3	243	8.4
1923–1924...	1,898	100.0	1,411	74.3	264	13.9	223	11.8
1924–1925...	1,983	100.0	1,392	70.2	272	13.7	319	16.1
1925–1926...	2,034	100.0	1,434	70.5	282	13.9	318	15.6

[a] The twelve-month period in each case is from December to November of the following year, inclusive.

TABLE XXV. LENGTH OF SERVICE IN A MEAT-PACKING ESTABLISHMENT OF SEPARATED EMPLOYEES WHO WERE LAID OFF, DECEMBER 2, 1922, TO NOVEMBER 27, 1926, INCLUSIVE; NUMBER AND PER CENT DISTRIBUTION

YEAR[a]	TOTAL		UNDER 3 MONTHS		3 TO 6 MONTHS		OVER 6 MONTHS	
	Number	Per cent Distribution	Number	Per cent Distribution	Number	Per cent Distribution	Number	Per cent Distribution
1922–1923...	520	100.0	428	82.3	76	14.6	16	3.1
1923–1924...	861	100.0	540	62.7	182	21.2	139	16.1
1924–1925...	754	100.0	382	50.7	200	26.5	172	22.8
1925–1926...	1,111	100.0	732	65.9	199	17.9	180	16.2

[a] The twelve-month period in each case is from December to November of the following year, inclusive.

TABLE XXVI. LENGTH OF SERVICE IN A MEAT-PACKING ESTABLISHMENT OF SEPARATED EMPLOYEES WHO WERE DISCHARGED, DECEMBER 2, 1922, TO NOVEMBER 27, 1926, INCLUSIVE; NUMBER AND PER CENT DISTRIBUTION

YEAR[a]	TOTAL		UNDER 3 MONTHS		3 TO 6 MONTHS		OVER 6 MONTHS	
	Number	Per cent Distribution	Number	Per cent Distribution	Number	Per cent Distribution	Number	Per cent Distribution
1922–1923...	1,018	100.0	866	85.1	103	10.1	49	4.8
1923–1924...	558	100.0	400	71.7	80	14.3	78	14.0
1924–1925...	501	100.0	413	82.4	40	8.0	48	9.6
1925–1926...	429	100.0	341	79.5	45	10.5	43	10.0

[a] The twelve-month period in each case is from December to November of the following year, inclusive.

stability. Chart XIV shows that white women left after about two years of service, or remained for a considerably longer period. One-third of all the Negro women held service records of three but under four years. These unskilled women workers hold better service records than might be expected. The record of the white women presents no unusual situation. The Negroes, while distributed among the higher service groups, fall off appreciably before completing four years of service, and raise a nice point of inquiry as to the reason for such a large percentage of them leaving during their fourth year.

The preceding analysis substantiates the packers' criticism of the high 'turnover' rate of Negro employees as a group. A comparison of the two groups by sex shows that the rate of mobility and replacement was higher in the majority of cases for the Negro men and women. During the four-year period, there was marked improvement in the rate of mobility of each group. The high rate of labor change was particularly true during the period of greatest industrial activity and the annual peak of employment. The intimate relationship between instability, the state of the labor market, the type of occupation, and the sex of workers has been shown. Industrial expansion and a tight labor market for

CHART XIV

LENGTH OF SERVICE IN A MEAT-PACKING ESTABLISHMENT
OF WOMEN EMPLOYEES

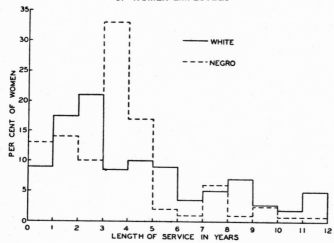

NUMBER AND PER CENT DISTRIBUTION AND CUMULATIVE PERCENTAGES

LENGTH OF SERVICE IN YEARS	WHITE			NEGRO		
	Num-ber	Per cent Distri-bution	Cumu-lative Per-centage	Num-ber	Per cent Distri-bution	Cumu-lative Per-centage
Total...................	241	100.0		123	100.0	
Under 1 year..............	22	9.1	9.1	16	13.0	13.0
1 and under 2 years......	42	17.4	26.5	17	13.8	26.8
2 and under 3 years......	51	21.2	47.7	12	9.8	36.6
3 and under 4 years......	20	8.3	56.0	41	33.3	69.9
4 and under 5 years......	24	10.0	66.0	21	17.1	87.0
5 and under 6 years......	22	9.1	75.1	2	1.6	88.6
6 and under 7 years......	7	2.9	78.0	1	.8	89.4
7 and under 8 years......	12	5.0	83.0	7	5.7	95.1
8 and under 9 years......	17	7.0	90.0	1	.8	95.9
9 and under 10 years......	6	2.5	92.5	3	2.5	98.4
10 and under 11 years......	4	1.7	94.2	1	.8	99.2
11 years and over..........	11	4.6	98.8	1	.8	100.0
Not reported..............	3	1.2	100.0	—	—	—

white workers accelerated the rate of labor changes among Negroes. The colored employees were frequently recent migrants from the South, totally ignorant of industry and of urban life, and in addition overconfident of obtaining employment. The yearly labor changes were a composite in the extremes of the monthly fluctuations of employment in the very seasonal work of the establishment. In addition, this annual increase of mobility and replacement during the establishment's busy season doubtless reflects not only increased industrial opportunities, but also a lack of industrial experience, training, and efficiency, true at least for part of the new colored recruits.

These considerations, when combined with the findings of previous sections showing occupational distribution and the management's preference for white workers, practically leave the fundamental question in regard to the steadiness and reliability—the rate of 'turnover'—of the Negro workman unanswered. The rate of the separations (voluntary quits, lay-offs, and discharges) from the establishment per full-year worker, and the length of service of employees, contribute an additional element of uncertainty. For, whereas quitting is generally the outstanding cause of the separations of the unskilled workers from any establishment or industry, this was not the case here. Negro men and women, the majority of whom occupied semi-skilled or unskilled positions, did not leave for this cause any more frequently than for lay-offs. Quitting, on the other hand, was the outstanding cause of the separations of the white workmen, who, moreover, maintained a higher rate of voluntary leaving than the Negroes. The reduction in the separation rates of Negroes compared favorably with or exceeded that shown by the white workers. And finally, excessive labor mobility was concentrated within a few months of each year and largely confined to the more recent accessions to the payroll.

The findings of the chapter raise, therefore, further points of inquiry involved in establishing conclusively the comparative industrial efficiency of white and Negro employees when measured by labor mobility. Is the Negro employee as capable of controlling his rate of mobility as the white?

Do the rates of labor change measure to the same degree the individual capacity of the white and Negro worker to 'stick by' a job? Are annual seasonal lay-offs the inevitable accompaniment of the occupations performed by Negroes? To what extent are racial considerations a factor in the situation? The most obvious generalizations are added in lieu of answers to these questions. The shiftlessness and unreliability of individual colored workmen have not been conclusively demonstrated. Unskilled laborers, in an establishment where work is seasonal, accept a high rate of 'turnover' as inevitable. Within this establishment the majority of the semi-skilled and common laborers are Negroes. The preference evidenced by the management for white workmen and the resulting fixed percentage of Negroes eligible for employment tend to perpetuate the situation.

APPENDICES

APPENDIX A

GENERAL TABLES XXVII–XXXII

TABLE XXVII. SLAUGHTERING AND MEAT-PACKING, SUMMARY FOR CHICAGO, 1889 TO 1925

YEAR	NUMBER OF ESTABLISHMENTS	WAGE-EARNERS (average number)*	CAPITAL†	WAGES†	COST OF MATERIALS†	VALUE OF PRODUCTS†	VALUE ADDED BY MANUFACTURE†
1925[a]	52	25,264	(j)	$35,319	$478,843	$ 571,052	$ 92,209[l]
1923[b]	50	30,382	(j)	39,334	(k)	514,667	(k)
1921[c]	41	27,209	(j)	35,219	394,773	452,572	57,799[l]
1919[d]	46	45,695	$395,716	69,864	957,786	1,083,090	125,304
1914[e]	37	26,408	194,434	16,311	342,508	406,983	64,475
1909[f]	—	—	—	—	—	—	—
1904[g]	32	22,613	70,265	12,388	237,039	269,581	32,542[l]
1899[h]	38	25,345	67,138	12,876	218,241	256,528	38,287[l]
1889[i]	57	17,875	39,222	11,006	173,568	203,606	30,038[l]

* The Census Bureau derives the average number of wage-earners by dividing the sum of the number employed on the 15th of each month by 12.

† Expressed in thousands of dollars.

[a] United States Bureau of the Census, *Census of Manufactures, Statistics for Industries, States and Cities*, 1925, p. 113. Figures for 1921, 1923, and 1925 do not include data for establishments reporting products valued at less than $5,000.

[b] United States Bureau of the Census, *Biennial Census of Manufactures*, 1923, p. 1402.

[c] United States Bureau of the Census, *Biennial Census of Manufactures*, 1921, p. 1536.

[d] United States Bureau of the Census, *Fourteenth Census of the United States*, 1920, IX, pp. 364-65.

[e] United States Bureau of the Census, *Census of Manufactures*, 1914, I, pp. 358-59.

[f] Separate statistics for 'slaughtering and meat-packing' are not available; the census designation for 1909 covered the three classes of establishments for which separate statistics were published for the three censuses of 1889, 1899, and 1904.

[g] Compiled from United States Bureau of the Census, *Special Reports of the Census Office*, 1905, Part II, pp. 236-37.

[h] Compiled from United States Bureau of the Census, *Twelfth Census of the United States* 1900, VIII, Part II, pp. 184-85.

[i] Compiled from United States Bureau of the Census, *Eleventh Census of the United States*, 1890, Part II, pp. 142-45. The data for 1889 are not strictly comparable with those of subsequent years because of changes in classification.

[j] Not called for on schedule.

[k] No data.

[l] Compiled, value of products less cost of materials.

TABLE XXVIII. SLAUGHTERING AND MEAT-PACKING, ALL BRANCHES COMBINED, SUMMARY FOR CHICAGO, 1879 to 1925, AND FOR COOK COUNTY, 1869

YEAR	NUMBER OF ESTAB-LISH-MENTS	WAGE-EARNERS (average number)	CAPITAL*	WAGES*	COST OF MATE-RIALS*	VALUE OF PROD-UCTS*	VALUE ADDED BY MANU-FACTURE*
1925[a]	94	26,371	([l])	$36,916	$492,314	$ 589,311	$ 96,997[n]
1923[b]	93	31,524	([l])	40,996	([m])	530,856	([m])
1921[c]	84	28,025	([l])	36,322	402,686	463,843	61,157[n]
1919[d]	95	46,474	$398,828	71,014	965,107	1,092,908	127,801
1914[e]	58	26,704	195,174	16,542	345,522	410,709	65,187
1909[f]	67	22,064	115,312	11,985	285,250	325,062	39,812
1904[g]	56	22,767	70,517	12,483	237,754	270,549	32,795[n]
1899[h]	52	25,478	67,314	12,948	218,739	257,276	38,537[n]
1889[i]	68	17,923	39,259	11,031	173,738	203,825	30,087[n]
1879[j]	70	7,478	8,455	3,393	74,546	85,324	10,778[n]
1869[k]	31	2,129	6,361	426	16,280	19,154	2,874[n]

* Expressed in thousands of dollars.
[a] Compiled from United States Bureau of the Census, *Census of Manufactures, Statistics for Industries, States and Cities*, 1925, p. 113. Figures for 1921, 1923, and 1925 do not include data for establishments reporting products valued at less than $5,000.
[b] Compiled from United States Bureau of the Census, *Biennial Census of Manufactures*, 1923, p. 1402.
[c] Compiled from United States Bureau of the Census, *Biennial Census of Manufactures*, 1921, p. 1536.
[d] Compiled from United States Bureau of the Census, *Fourteenth Census of the United States*, 1920, IX, pp. 364-65.
[e] Compiled from United States Bureau of the Census, *Census of Manufactures*, 1914, I, pp. 358-59.
[f] United States Bureau of the Census, *Thirteenth Census of the United States*, 1910 IX, pp. 298-99.
[g] Compiled from United States Bureau of the Census, *Special Reports of the Census Office*, 1905, Part II, pp. 236-37.
[h] Compiled from United States Bureau of the Census, *Twelfth Census of the United States*, 1900, VIII, Part II, pp. 184-85.
[i] Compiled from United States Bureau of the Census, *Eleventh Census of the United States*, 1890, Part II, pp. 142-45. The data for 1889 and previous years are not strictly comparable with those of subsequent years because of changes in classification.
[j] United States Bureau of the Census, *Tenth Census of the United States*, 1880, II, p. 393.
[k] United States Bureau of the Census, *Ninth Census of the United States, Industry and Wealth*, 1870, III, p. 649. In 1869 the statistics were collected for Cook County under the heading 'Meat Packed Pork.'
[l] Not called for on schedule.
[m] No data.
[n] Compiled, value of products less cost of materials.

TABLE XXIX. SLAUGHTERING AND MEAT-PACKING, SUMMARY FOR ILLINOIS, 1889 to 1925

YEAR	NUMBER OF ESTAB-LISH-MENTS	WAGE-EARNERS (average number)	CAPITAL*	WAGES*	COST OF MATE-RIALS*	VALUE OF PROD-UCTS*	VALUE ADDED BY MANU-FACTURE*
1925[a]	78	30,236	(j)	$41,467	$ 570,538	$ 680,592	$110,054
1923[b]	78	36,144	(j)	46,174	509,744	606,321	96,577
1921[c]	63	32,136	(j)	41,616	455,745	527,509	71,764
1919[d]	72	54,179	$430,376	79,983	1,142,950	1,284,103	141,153
1914[e]	70	31,315	210,561	19,286	408,895	485,362	76,467
1909[f]	75	26,344	(k)	14,356	341,348	386,366	45,018[l]
1904[g]	68	26,953	80,477	14,561	279,855	317,206	37,351[l]
1899[h]	64	27,861	71,229	14,045	246,713	287,922	41,209[l]
1889[i]	81	18,916	40,807	11,587	180,904	212,291	31,387[l]

* Expressed in thousands of dollars.
  [a] United States Bureau of the Census, *Census of Manufactures, Slaughtering and Meat-Packing*, 1925, pp. 19-20. Figures for 1921, 1923, and 1925 do not include data for establishments reporting products valued at less than $5,000.
  [b] United States Bureau of the Census, *Census of Manufactures, Slaughtering and Meat-Packing*, 1923, pp. 17-18.
  [c] United States Bureau of the Census, *Biennial Census of Manufactures*, 1921, p. 1399.
  [d] United States Bureau of the Census, *Fourteenth Census of the United States*, 1920, IX, pp. 356-57.
  [e] United States Bureau of the Census, *Census of Manufactures*, 1914, I, pp. 350-51.
  [f] United States Bureau of the Census, *Census of Manufactures*, 1914, II, p. 337.
  [g] Compiled from United States Bureau of the Census, *Special Reports of the Census Office, Manufactures*, 1905, Part II, pp. 228-29.
  [h] Compiled from United States Bureau of the Census, *Twelfth Census of the United States*, 1900, VIII, Part II, pp. 176-77.
  [i] Compiled from United States Bureau of the Census, *Eleventh Census of the United States*, 1890, Part I, pp. 394-95. The data for 1889 are not strictly comparable with those of subsequent years because of changes in classification.
  [j] Not called for on schedule.
  [k] No data.
  [l] Compiled, value of products less cost of materials.

TABLE XXX. SLAUGHTERING AND MEAT-PACKING, ALL BRANCHES COMBINED, SUMMARY FOR ILLINOIS, 1869 to 1925

YEAR	NUMBER OF ESTABLISHMENTS	WAGE-EARNERS (average number)	CAPITAL*	WAGES*	COST OF MATERIALS*	VALUE OF PRODUCTS*	VALUE ADDED BY MANUFACTURE*
1925[a]	129	31,401	(j)	$43,169	$ 584,737	$ 699,862	$113,125
1923[b]	130	37,329	(j)	47,907	521,895	623,114	101,219
1921[c]	113	32,976	(j)	42,752	463,851	539,048	75,197
1919[d]	126	54,975	$433,547	81,160	1,150,463	1,294,167	143,704
1914[e]	98	31,627	211,334	19,532	412,015	489,230	77,215
1909[f]	109	26,705	131,026	14,602	343,976	389,595	45,619
1904[f]	95	27,111	80,733	14,658	280,592	318,201	37,609
1899[f]	78	27,991	71,394	14,115	247,215	288,672	41,457
1889[g]	94	18,972	40,851	11,618	181,087	212,539	31,452[k]
1879[h]	143	10,948	12,020	4,078	84,650	97,892	13,242[k]
1869[i]	59	2,626	7,498	600	20,214	24,071	3,857[k]

* Expressed in thousands of dollars.
[a] Compiled from United States Bureau of the Census, *Census of Manufactures, Slaughtering and Meat-Packing*, 1925, pp. 19-20, 24. Figures for 1921, 1923, and 1925 do not include data for establishments reporting products valued at less than $5,000.
[b] Compiled from United States Bureau of the Census, *Biennial Census of Manufactures*, 1923, p. 1275.
[c] Compiled from United States Bureau of the Census, *Biennial Census of Manufactures*, 1921, p. 1399.
[d] Compiled from United States Bureau of the Census, *Fourteenth Census of the United States*, 1920, IX, pp. 356-57.
[e] Compiled from United States Bureau of the Census, *Census of Manufactures*, 1914, I, pp. 350-51.
[f] United States Bureau of the Census, *Thirteenth Census of the United States*, 1910, VIII, p. 635.
[g] Compiled from United States Bureau of the Census, *Eleventh Census of the United States*, 1890, Part I, pp. 394-95. The data for 1889 and previous years are not strictly comparable with those of subsequent years because of changes in classification.
[h] United States Bureau of the Census, *Tenth Census of the United States, Statistics of Manufactures*, 1880, II, p. 111.
[i] Compiled from United States Bureau of the Census, *Ninth Census of the United States, Industry and Wealth*, 1870, III, pp. 510-11.
[j] Not called for on schedule.
[k] Compiled, value of products less cost of materials.

TABLE XXXI. SLAUGHTERING AND MEAT-PACKING, SUMMARY FOR THE UNITED STATES, 1849 to 1925

YEAR	NUMBER OF ESTAB-LISH-MENTS	WAGE-EARNERS (average number)	CAPITAL*	WAGES*	COST OF MATE-RIALS*	VALUE OF PROD-UCTS*	VALUE ADDED BY MANU-FACTURE*
1925[a]	1,269	120,422	([e])	$159,355	$2,625,192	$3,050,286	$425,094
1923[a]	1,397	132,792	([e])	167,569	2,176,010	2,585,804	409,794
1921[b]	1,184	117,042	([e])	152,903	1,868,198	2,200,942	332,744
1919[b]	1,304	160,996	$1,176,484	209,489	3,782,930	4,246,291	463,361
1914[b]	1,279	98,832	534,274	62,136	1,441,663	1,651,965	210,302
1909[b]	1,221	87,813	378,319	50,404	1,191,438	1,355,544	164,106
1904[b]	929	74,134	237,715	40,327	805,857	913,915	108,058
1899[b]	882	68,386	188,800	33,392	682,097	783,779	101,682
1889[b]	1,118	43,975	116,888	24,305	480,962	561,612	80,650
1879[b]	872	27,297	49,419	10,509	267,739	303,562	35,823
1869[b]	768	8,366	24,225	2,553	61,674	75,827	14,153
1859[b]	259	5,058	10,158	1,019	23,564	29,442	5,878
1849[b]	185	3,276	3,483	1,232	9,451	11,982	2,531

* Expressed in thousands of dollars.

[a] United States Bureau of the Census, *Census of Manufactures, Slaughtering and Meat-Packing*, 1925, p. 6. Data for establishments with products under $5,000 in value are not included for 1921, 1923, and 1925. This change resulted in a 21.6 per cent reduction in the number of establishments in regard to which general and detailed statistics were compiled at the census of 1921. In no other respect is the comparability of biennial and quinquennial figures impaired, since 99.4 per cent of the total wage-earners and 99.7 per cent of the total value of products reported at that census were contributed by establishments having products valued at $5,000 or more.

[b] United States Bureau of the Census, *Census of Manufactures, Slaughtering and Meat-Packing*, 1921, p. 6. The data for 1889 and previous years are not strictly comparable with those of 1899 and subsequent years, due to changes in classification.

[e] Not called for on schedule for 1921, 1923, 1925.

TABLE XXXII. SLAUGHTERING AND MEAT-PACKING, ALL BRANCHES COMBINED, SUMMARY FOR THE UNITED STATES, 1849 to 1925

YEAR	NUMBER OF ESTAB-LISH-MENTS	WAGE-EARNERS (average number)	CAPITAL*	WAGES*	COST OF MATE-RIALS*	VALUE OF PROD-UCTS*	VALUE ADDED BY MANU-FACTURE*
1925[a]	1,758	125,336	(d)	$167,007	$2,686,690	$3,132,722	$446,032
1923[a]	1,896	137,384	(d)	174,409	2,227,044	2,655,315	428,271
1921[a]	1,697	120,914	(d)	158,382	1,905,640	2,254,029	348,389
1919[a]	1,937	164,467	—	214,168	3,826,870	4,302,901	476,031
1914[a]	1,812	101,448	—	63,957	1,459,588	1,675,048	215,460
1909[b]	1,641	89,728	$383,249	51,645	1,202,828	1,370,568	167,740
1904[b]	1,221	75,399	240,419	41,067	811,426	922,038	110,612
1899[b]	1,080	69,264	190,209	33,846	685,310	788,368	103,058
1889[b]	1,367	44,812	118,016	24,668	482,897	564,667	81,770
1879[c]	872	27,297	49,419	10,509[e]	267,739	303,562	35,823
1869[c]	768	8,366	24,225	2,553[e]	61,674	75,827	14,153
1859[c]	259	5,058	10,158	1,019[e]	23,564	29,442	5,878
1849[c]	185	3,276	3,483	1,232[e]	9,451	11,982	2,531

* Expressed in thousands of dollars.
[a] Compiled from United States Bureau of the Census, *Census of Manufactures, Slaughtering and Meat-Packing,* 1925, pp. 6, 21. Figures for 1921, 1923, and 1925 do not include data for establishments reporting products valued at less than $5,000.
[b] United States Bureau of the Census, *Thirteenth Census of the United States,* 1910, X, p. 334.
[c] United States Bureau of the Census, *Census of Manufactures, Slaughtering and Meat-Packing,* 1921, p. 6. The data for 1889 and previous years are not strictly comparable with those of 1899 and subsequent years because of changes in classification.
[d] Not called for on schedule.
[e] Includes salaries.

APPENDIX B

COPIES OF SERVICE RECORDS OF WHITE AND NEGRO WOMEN

NEGRO WOMAN

Date of Entrance	Department	Position	Hourly Wage Rate	Date of Leaving	Reason
4–10–18	Hair	Rope weaving	.24½		
7–22–18	Beef Casing				
	Hog Head	Casing grading	.34		
9–14–20	Hog Head	Casing grading	.42		
11–25–20	Hog Head	Casing grading	.42		
5–9–21	Hair	Rope weaving	.31		
5–26–21	Hog Head	Trim tongues	.31	5–30–21	Transferred
6–4–21	Hog Killing	Trim cheek	.31		
8–16–21		Save lung	.31		
8–24–21	Hog Head	Split bone	.31	8–25–25	Laid off
10–15–21	Hog Head	Wash chitterlings	.31		
2–27–22	Hog Killing	Wash chitterlings	.25	8–24–22	
8–30–22	Lard Refining	Wrapper	.25		
10–9–22	Casing Packing	Grader	.25		

WHITE WOMAN

Date of Entrance	Department	Position	Hourly Wage Rate	Date of Leaving	Reason
8–28–22	Pork Trimming	Trimming	.25		
5–24–23	Pork Trimming	Inspecting	.30	8–21–23	Laid off, no work
9–24–23	Summer Sausage	Scrape casings	.30	12–12–23	Discharged
7–11–24	Hog Killing	Wash chitterlings	.30	7–22–24	Laid off, no work
7–29–24	Hog Killing	Wash chitterlings	.30	2–4–25	Laid off, no work
3–3–25	Bone House	Dry blood albumin	.35	4–6–25	Laid off, no work
5–2–25	Hog Head	Wash chitterlings	.30	6–25–25	Transferred
	Hog Head	Save brains	.36	7–21–25	Transferred
	Hog Head	Wash chitterlings	.30	2–3–26	Transferred
	Hog Head	Save brains	.36	3–5–26	Transferred
3–5–26	Hog Killing	Wash chitterlings	.30		

NEGRO WOMAN

Date of Entrance	Department	Position	Hourly Wage Rate	Date of Leaving	Reason
11–17–18	Beef Casing	Pack fat	.20½	12–1919	Changed number
	Beef Tallow	Pack fat	.30½	1–4–22	Transferred
1–4–22	Beef Casing	Inspecting	.37½		

NEGRO WOMAN

Date of Entrance	Department	Position	Hourly Wage Rate	Date of Leaving	Reason
1922	Lard Pail	Bailing	.25		
1923	Lard Pail	Bailing	.30		
1923	Lard Pail	Lock seamer	.33		
1924	Lard Pail	Ear press	.37 } and		Laid off, no work
1924	Lard Pail	General work	.30 }		
1924	Lard Pail	Lock seamer	.33		
1925	Lard Pail	General work	.30		
	Lard Pail	Body press	.33		
1925	Lard Pail	Body press	.33		
1926	Lard Pail	Body press	.30		

WHITE WOMAN

Date of Entrance	Department	Position	Hourly Wage Rate	Date of Leaving	Reason
4-3-17	Beef Casings	Pack fat	.34	5-31-18	Not here
7-8-18	Beef Casings	Pack fat	.36½	10-3-19	Father ill
10-28-19	Beef Casings	Pack fat	.36½		
	Beef Casings	Pack fat	.46	6-7-21	Resigned to be married
8-16-21	Mutton Tallow	Save fat	.31	9-23-21	Transferred
9-23-21	Beef Tallow	Save fat	.31	11-16-21	Transferred
11-16-21	Mutton Tallow	Save fat	.31	2-27-22	Change Number
2-27-22	Mutton Tallow	Save fat	.34	3-26-25	Transferred
3-26-25	Beef Casing	Inspector	.42½		

NEGRO WOMAN

Date of Entrance	Department	Position	Hourly Wage Rate	Date of Leaving	Reason
7-8-22	Casing Packing	Grader	.25	7-12-22	Transfer
7-12-22	Beef Tallow	Pack fat	.25	8-30-22	Transfer
8-30-22	Beef Killing	Save feet	.30	4-28-26	Change of rates
4-28-27	Beef Killing	Save feet	.33		

WHITE WOMAN

Date of Entrance	Department	Position	Hourly Wage Rate	Date of Leaving	Reason
1916	Lard Pail	General work	.10		
1916			.12½		
1916			.15½		
1917			.17½		
1917			.20		
1918			.24½		
1918			.30½		
1919			.33	1920	Laid off, no work
1920	Bailing		.42		
1921	Bailing		.34		
	Bailing		.34	1921	Laid off, no work
1921	Lard Pail	Bailing	.25		
1923	Lard Pail	Bailing	.30	1923	Laid off, no work
1923	Lard Pail	General work	.30		
1924	Lard Pail	General work	.30	1924	Laid off, no work
1924	Lard Pail	General work	.30		

Negro Woman

Date of Entrance	Department	Position	Hourly Wage Rate	Date of Leaving	Reason
12–1–22	Lard Pail	General work	.25	12–2–22	Didn't like work
2–5–23	Tin Shop	General work	.25		
4–16–23	Tin Shop	General work	.30		

White Woman

Date of Entrance	Department	Position	Hourly Wage Rate	Date of Leaving	Reason
10–5–18	Sausage	Twisting franks	.33	12–5–19	Dropped, laid off
12–16–19	Sausage	Twisting franks	.33		
5–8–20	Sausage	Twisting franks	.42	10–30–20	Laid off
1–31–21	Sausage	Twisting franks	.42		
3–19–21	Sausage	Twisting franks	.34		
12–3–21	Sausage	Twisting franks	.28	12–9–21	Strike
12–13–21	Sausage	Twisting franks	.28		
4–16–23	Sausage	Twisting franks	.33	2–7–25	
3–16–25	Sausage	Twisting franks	.32½		

Negro Woman

Date of Entrance	Department	Position	Hourly Wage Rate	Date of Leaving	Reason
1919		Stacking	.33	1919	Dropped, laid off slack
1920		Stacking	.33		
1920		Single automatic press	.33		
1920		Single automatic press	.42		
1920		Double automatic press	.42 .43½ } and		Laid off, slack
1921	Tin Shop	Single press	.34		
1921	Tin Shop	Single press	.34 .36 } and		
1921	Tin Shop	Single press	.30 .28 } and		
1921	Tin Shop	Single press	.30 .28 } and		
1922	Tin Shop	Single press	.30 .28 } and		
1922	Tin Shop	Ear machine	.28 .32 } and		
1923	Tin Shop	Ear machine	.33 .37 } and		

White Woman

Date of Entrance	Department	Position	Hourly Wage Rate	Date of Leaving	Reason
5–2–23	Round Can	General work	.30	8–25–23	Laid off
10–9–23	Label Room	General work	.30		
5–10–26	Label Room	General work	.30		

WHITE WOMAN

Date of Entrance	Department	Position	Hourly Wage Rate	Date of Leaving	Reason
7–17–16	Tin Shop	Stacking	.10	2–5–17	Laid off
8–8–17	Tin Shop	Stacking	.20		
9–8–17	Tin Shop	Stacking	.22½		
9–12–18	Tin Shop	Stacking	.27		
10–11–18	Tin Shop	Stacking	.34	4–13–18	
9–15–19	Tin Shop	Stacking	.33	12–5–19	
12–15–19	Tin Shop	Stacking	.33		
5–8–20	Tin Shop	Stacking	.42		
3–19–21	Tin Shop	Stacking	.34		
12–3–21	Tin Shop	Stacking	.28	12–8–21	Strike
12–28–21	Tin Shop	Stacking	.28		
2–9–23	Tin Shop	Forelady	.30		
4–16–23	Tin Shop	Forelady	.35		

NEGRO WOMAN

Date of Entrance	Department	Position	Hourly Wage Rate	Date of Leaving	Reason
9–6–22	Tin Shop	Stacking	.25		
11–19–22	Tin Shop	Auto press	.27½	4–11–23	Better job
10–12–23	Tin Shop	General work	.30		
11–2–23	Tin Shop	Auto press	.32½		
1–4–24	Tin Shop	General work	.32½ and .30		
–7–24	Tin Shop	General work	.32½ and .30		
1–25–24	Tin Shop	General work	.30	2–8–24	Laid off, slack
11–16–25	Tin Shop	General work	.30		
12–19–25	Tin Shop	Auto press	.32½		

NEGRO WOMAN

Date of Entrance	Department	Position	Hourly Wage Rate	Date of Leaving	Reason
10–19–17	Pork Trimming	Trimming			
10–24–18	Fresh Pork	Pack		12–1–18	Not here
	Fresh Pork	Wrap loins		2–27–22	Changed work
	Pork Trimming	Trim and pack	.42½	10–16–23	Changed work
	Pork Trimming	Trim and pack	.42½	4–22–24	Change number
	Fresh Pork	Pack loins	.42½	9–29–24	Transfer
	Hog Killing	Wash chitterlings	.30	10–30–24	Transfer
	Fresh Pork	Pack loins	.42½	3–4–25	Transfer
	Hog Killing	Wash chitterlings	.30	5–24–25	Transfer
	Fresh Pork	Wrap loins	.42½	7–8–25	Transfer
	Hog Killing	Kidney puller	.30	12–3–25	Transfer
	Pork Packing	Wrap loins	.42½	2–25–26	Transfer
2–25–22	Hog Killing	Kidney puller	.30		

WHITE WOMAN

Date of Entrance	Department	Position	Hourly Wage Rate	Date of Leaving	Reason
3–8–20	Round Can	General labor	.33		
4–24–20			.33		
5–8–20			.42	7–20–20	Laid off
6–30–21	Round Can	General work	.34		
1–13–22	Round Can	General work	.25		
2–27–22	Sausage	General work	.25		
10–19–22	Sausage	Inspector	.27½		
4–16–23	Sausage	Inspector	.32½		
11–26–23	Square Can	Inspector	.32½		
2–25–24	Sausage	Inspector	.32½	9–27–24	
10–2–24	Square Can	Scaling	.32½		
11–19–24	Square Can	Scaling	.32½		
12–15–24	Sausage	Scaling	.32½		
12–22–24	Square Can	Scaling	.32½		
1–26–25	Round Can	Scaling	.32½		
4–27–25	Sausage	Scaling	.32½		
5–27–25	Square Can	Scaling	.32½		
8–17–25	Square Can	Scaling	.32½		
1–11–26	Sausage	Scaling	.32½		

NEGRO WOMAN

Date of Entrance	Department	Position	Hourly Wage Rate	Date of Leaving	Reason
12–15–19	Lard Pail	Bailing	.33		
5–8–20	Lard Pail	Bailing	.42		
6–28–20	Lard Pail	Bailing	.42		
12–7–21	Lard Pail	Bailing	.25		
	Lard Pail	Bailing	.25		
1–3–22	Lard Pail	Bailing	.25		
2–13–22	Lard Pail	Bailing	.25		
4–16–23	Lard Pail	General work	.30	11–30–23	
7–23–24	Tin Shop	General work	.30		

NEGRO WOMAN

Date of Entrance	Department	Position	Hourly Wage Rate	Date of Leaving	Reason
10–16–19	Round Can	General work	.33		
11–6–19	Round Can	Capper	.36½		
1–3–20			.36½		
5–8–20			.46		
12–8–20			.46		
3–19–21			.38		
12–3–21	Round Can		.32		
2–6–22	Round Can		.32		
11–6–22	Round Can	Laundry	.35		
1–5–23	Round Can	Laundry	.35		
4–16–23	Round Can	Laundry	.40		
11–5–25	Round Can	Clerk	.42½		

NEGRO WOMAN

Date of Entrance	Department	Position	Hourly Wage Rate	Date of Leaving	Reason
8–13–23	Label Room	General work	.30		

NEGRO WOMAN

Date of Entrance	Department	Position	Hourly Wage Rate	Date of Leaving	Reason
1922	Lard Pail	Passing parts	.25		
1922	Lard Pail	Lock seamer	.28		
1923	Lard Pail	Lock seamer	.33		Temporary absence
1923	Lard Pail	Lock seamer	.33		reinstated
1924	Lard Pail	Stack cans	.30 .33 } and		

WHITE WOMAN

Date of Entrance	Department	Position	Hourly Wage Rate	Date of Leaving	Reason
5–8–20		Cutting frankfurters	.42	11–2–20	
3–19–21		Cutting frankfurters	.42		
11–7–21	Sausage	Cutting frankfurters	.34		
11–7–21	Sausage	Cutting frankfurters	.34		
12–3–21	Sausage	Cutting frankfurters	.28	12–7–21	Strike
1–7–21					Returned
4–16–23	Sausage	Washing casings	.30		

WHITE WOMAN

Date of Entrance	Department	Position	Hourly Wage Rate	Date of Leaving	Reason
1921	Lard Pail	General work	.34		Slack
	Lard Pail	General work	.34	1921	Off
1921	Square Can	General work	.34		
1921	Square Can	General work	.28		Slack
	Square Can	General work	.28	1921	Off
1922	Tin Shop	Stacking	.25		Slack
	Tin Shop	Stacking		1922	Off
1922	Round Can	General work	.25		
1923	Round Can	General work	.30		Slack
1925	Sausage	General work	.30	1926	Off
1926	Lard Pail	General work	.30		

WHITE WOMAN

Date of Entrance	Department	Position	Hourly Wage Rate	Date of Leaving	Reason
10–10–19	Sausage	Scaler	.33	12–6–19	
12–16–19			.33		
5–8–20			.42		
6–28–20			.42		
7–30–20		Scaler	.42	11–2–20	
			.46		
1–17–21		General work	.42		
3–19–21			.34	12–8–21	Strike
12–19–21					Returned
1–6–22	Sausage	Scaler	.28 .32 } and		
4–16–23	Sausage	Scaler	.32 .37 } and		

NEGRO WOMAN

Date of Entrance	Department	Position	Hourly Wage Rate	Date of Leaving	Reason
5–31–22	Lard Pail	Inspecting cans	.25		
	Lard Pail	Lock seamer	.28		
	Lard Pail	Lock seamer	.28	9–14–22	
6–6–23	Lard Pail	General work	.30		
6–15–23	Lard Pail	Cover press	.35	7–21–23	
7–26–23	Lard Pail	General work	.30		
8–17–23	Lard Pail	Body press	.33		
1–4–24	Lard Pail	Stacking cans	.30 and .33		
5–7–24	Tin Shop	Stacking cans	.30		
7–21–24	Lard Pail	Stacking cans	.30		
8–9–24	Lard Pail	Body press	.30 and .33		
9–30–24	Tin Shop	General work	.30		
12–11–24	Tin Shop	General work	.30	1–13–26	
1–19–26	Tin Shop	General work	.30		
1–23–26	Tin Shop	General work	.30		

WHITE WOMAN

Date of Entrance	Department	Position	Hourly Wage Rate	Date of Leaving	Reason
4–17–19		Vacuum machine	.33		
8–21–19			.36½	12–20–19	
2–3–20		Vacuum machine	.36½		
5–8–20		Vacuum machine	.46	10–19–20	
1–7–21		General work	.42	4–5–21	
8–25–21	Square Can	Vacuum machine	.38		
12–3–21	Square Can	Vacuum machine	.32		
	Square Can	Vacuum machine	.32	12–7–21	
9–18–22	Square Can	Vacuum machine	.25 and .27½	and	
10–2–22	Square Can	Vacuum machine	.27½		
	Square Can	Vacuum machine	.27½		
3–27–23	Round Can	Vacuum machine	.27½		
4–16–23	Round Can	Vacuum machine	.32½		
8–27–23	Square Can	Vacuum machine	.32½		
1–17–24	Square Can	General work	.32½ and .30	and	
1–28–24	Square Can	General work	.30		
2–25–24	Dried Beef	General work	.30		
3–8–24	Round Can	General work	.30	4–5–24	
8–11–24	Round Can	General work	.30		
8–18–24	Square Can	General work	.30		
9–26–24	Square Can	Stuffing	.32½		
1–26–25	Sausage	Stuffing	.32½		
9–14–25	Square Can	Stuffing	.32½		
1–11–26	Sausage	Stuffing	.32½		

NEGRO WOMAN

Date of Entrance	Department	Position	Hourly Wage Rate	Date of Leaving	Reason
8–16–21	Lard Pail	Bailing	.34		
	Lard Pail	Bailing	.34	10–22–21	
12–23–21	Press Room	Stacking	.25		
2–13–22	Press Room	Stacking	.25		
4–16–23	Press Room	Stacking	.30		

NEGRO WOMAN

Date of Entrance	Department	Position	Hourly Wage Rate	Date of Leaving	Reason
2-8-23	Label Room	General work	.25		
4-16-23	Label Room	General work	.30		

NEGRO WOMAN

Date of Entrance	Department	Position	Hourly Wage Rate	Date of Leaving	Reason
7-25-22	Lard Pail	Bailing	.25		
8-7-22	Lard Pail	Bailing	.25		
4-16-23	Lard Pail	Bailing	.30	5-10-23	Discharged
6-21-23	Lard Pail	General work	.30		
8-3-23	Lard Pail	Auto press	.32½		
8-8-23	Tin Shop	Auto press	.32½		
10-14-25	Tin Shop	Auto press	.32½		

NEGRO WOMAN

Date of Entrance	Department	Position	Hourly Wage Rate	Date of Leaving	Reason
5-20-18	Canned Dried Beef	General work	.33		
5-8-20	Canned Dried Beef	General work	.42		
12-4-20	Canned Dried Beef	General work	.42	12-14-20	Laid off
6-23-21	Canned Dried Beef	Washing jars	.34		
12-3-21	Canned Dried Beef	Washing jars	.28		
4-16-23	Canned Dried Beef	Washing jars	.33		

WHITE WOMAN

Date of Entrance	Department	Position	Hourly Wage Rate	Date of Leaving	Reason
11-18-20	Pork Trimming	Trimmer	.44	12-15-20	Laid off
1-10-21	Pork Trimming	Trimmer	.44		
2-21-21	Pork Trimming	Trimmer	.39		
4-21-21	Pork Trimming	Piece-work		12-23-21	Changed work
1-3-22	Pork Trimming	Piece-work			
2-27-22	Pork Trimming	Trimmer Piece-work		10-15-24	
	Hog Killing	Wash chitterlings	.30	10-30-24	
	⌠Pork Trimming	Trimmer		3-4-25	
	⌡Hog Killing	Kidney puller	.30	6-24-25	Transfer
	Pork Trimming	Trimming Piece-work		7-8-25	Transfer
	Hog Killing	Wash chitterlings	.30	12-3-25	Transfer
	Pork Trimming	Trimmer Piece-work		2-25-26	Transfer
2-25-26	Hog Killing	Wash chitterlings	.30		

WHITE WOMAN

Date of Entrance	Department	Position	Hourly Wage Rate	Date of Leaving	Reason
1917	Sheep Casing				Transfer
3–27–18	Stuff	Stuffer	.30½	9–30–18	Did not notify when absent
	Stuff	Stuffer	.33	1–29–20	Did not notify when absent
1–30–20	Lard	Wipe cans	.33	2–11–20	Laid off, no work
2–19–20	Lard	Wipe cans	.33		
	Lard	Wipe cans	.33	2–27–20	Laid off, no work
6–7–20	Janitress	Clean nights	17.83		
6–15–20	Sausage manu-facturing	Wash pans	.45	6–28–20	Laid off
10–18–20	Summer Sausage	Trimmer	.42	2–16–21	Discharged
2–25–21	Smokehouse	Label and tie	.39		Laid off
3–10–21	Smokehouse	Label and tie	.39	3 ——	
3–18–21	Lard Refining	Changing	.31	3–29–21	Laid off
4–22–21	Hog Head	Stamp	.31	4–27–21	Laid off
5–16–21	Summer Sausage	Washer	.31		
6–8–21	Beef Casing		.31		
2–16–22	Summer Sausage	Trimmer	.25	2–17–22	Laid off
7–17–23	Sausage manu-facturing	Bung clipper	.30	7–12–23	Resigned
9–10–23	Beef Casing	Bung clipper	.42½		

APPENDIX C

DESCRIPTION OF CERTAIN OPERATIONS

The following 157 employees were required in slaughtering 1,050 cattle in a working-day of ten hours: 1 general foreman, 1 foreman over yard gang, 1 driving up cattle, 2 penning cattle, 2 knocking cattle, 2 shackling cattle, 1 hanging off for shackler, 1 squeezing blood from beds, 1 switching onto heading beds and putting up heads, 1 throwing down heads, 1 pritching up, 1 dropping cattle, 1 pritching up helper, 1 sticker, 3 headers, 1 ripper, 4 leg breakers, 3 feet skinners, 1 gullet raiser, 7 floormen, 1 breast sawyer, 1 aitch sawyer, 2½ caul pullers, 2 putting in hooks to hoists for fell cutter, 1 floor squeezer, 1 washing crutches and bellies, 4 fell cutters, 1 cutting out bladders, 2 rumpers, 1 rump helper and drop hide feller, 2 backers, 4 splitters, 1 back and rump hand, 1 washing hind shanks, 1 ripping tails and cutting out, 1 pulling tails, 2½ gutters, 2 throwing down guts and paunches, 3 tail sawyers, 2 hanging off from splitter, 3 beating out fells, 1 helper sawing tails and ripping open, 2 neck splitters, 1 tallow lot man, 1 trucking feet, 1 trucking up hooks, 1 hanging up hooks, 2 clearing out, 3 dropping hides.

Washing gang: 1 foreman, 1 trimming bruises on rail, 1 wiping beef, 1 putting in neck and kidney cloths, 1 scribe sawyer, 1 hoseman, 1 washing shanks, 1 switchman, 3 washing ribs and necks inside, 1 squeezing beef, 1 pumping kidneys, 3 long brush washers, 1 washing rags, 2 wiping hinds, 2 ladder men (knife), 2 bruise trimmers, 1 cutting off cords and shanks, 1 tying veins, 2 trimming skirts and necks, 1 pumping necks.

Weighing beef and helpers: 1 scaler, 1 grader, 1 pushing on scale or tagger, 1 pulling off scale, 1 elevator man.

Refrigerating and car loading: 14 beef coolers, 5 trimmers, 7 carriers and loaders, 11 laborers.

The following 63 employees were engaged in handling by-products:

Hide gang: 1 hide inspector, 2 spreading out hides, 2 trucking to chute.

Laborers downstairs: 1 throwing down paunches, 3 truckers, 2 peck machine hands, 1 taking off toes, 1 sawing shin bones, 1 handling livers, 1 sawing horns, 1 chopping brains, 1 offal lot hand, 1 ruffle man, 1 trimming glands (boy), 1 washing tongues, 1 washing weasands, 1 foreman, 1 bed tallow hand, 1 tripe washer, 1 squeezing, 1 scaler, 3 head boners.

Knife men downstairs: 1 cutting off pecks, 1 cutting off peck butter, 3 trimming paunches, 1 opening paunches, 3 handling pecks and trimming deeds, 1 trimming heart casings, 1 trimming small bungs.

Cooler department for offal, etc.: 12 cooler men, 1 scaler.

Offal department: 1 trimming livers, 1 cutting off tongues, 1 trimming tongues, 1 pulling weasands, 1 trimming plucks, 1 trimming hearts, 1 trimming cheek meat, 1 trimming small cheek meat, 1 trimming sweetbreads and tails, 1 cutting sinews.[1]

A summary of the departments and occupations found in studies made by the United States Bureau of Labor Statistics in 1917, 1921, 1923, 1925, and 1927 of the wages and hours in the slaughtering and meat-packing industry shows the same situation.[2] The method of enumeration by which various operations within the same department are grouped under a single occupational category, provided the rate of wages does not vary between them, reduces the number of operations. For the past ten years there have been only slight variations in the recorded number of departments and of occupations within the industry. The five studies mentioned are not identical as regards departmental enumeration, but the dissimilarities are of minor importance. In 1927, wages and hours of males are recorded for thirty-four occupations in cattle killing, fifteen in hog killing, twenty in sheep killing and calf killing, sixteen in offal (other than hides and casings), three in hide, twelve in casing, fourteen in cutting fresh beef, seventeen in cutting fresh pork, seven in lard and oleo oil, eleven in sausage, ten in cured meat, thirteen in canning, twenty-four in maintenance and repair,

[1] *Report of the Commissioner of Corporations on the Beef Industry*, March 3, 1905, pp. 17-18.
[2] United States Department of Labor, Bureau of Labor Statistics, *Wages and Hours of Labor in the Slaughtering and Meat-Packing Industry;* 1917, Bulletin No. 252; 1921, Bulletin No. 294; 1923, Bulletin No. 373; 1925, Bulletin No. 421; 1927, Bulletin No. 472.

and four miscellaneous occupations, all departments. The wages and hours for the females were tabulated for one occupation in the cattle killing department, one in hog-killing, nine in offal (other than hides and casings), nine in casing, one in cutting fresh beef, two in cutting fresh pork, one in lard and oleo oil, eight in sausage, one in cured meat, twelve in canning, and two miscellaneous occupations, all departments.[1]

How the operations actually work out in the various plants varies slightly. The division of labor has become standardized.[2] The following examples of minute subdivision in the industrial processes of the industry were found in 1928 in an establishment of national importance and are considered typical of those seen during the investigation. Description of operations in departments not ordinarily frequented by the plant visitor have been chosen for presentation. The hourly rate of wages paid and the sex and race of the person performing the operation will be given.

The hog head section is a corner of the general hog-killing room. The head is unjointed early in the dressing process, but left hanging in order that the Government inspector may examine the glands for tuberculosis or other disease. After the hog has progressed a considerable distance on the moving conveyor, along which workers stand each performing a given operation, the head is removed. The animal is now well on its way to the cooler, and the offal must have immediate and careful attention, for it spoils quickly. A Negro man, who removes the head and cuts out the tongue, receives 50 cents an hour. The head is skinned by a white man who receives 49 cents an hour. The same rate is paid for chiseling heads and templing them, marking snouts, cutting off lips, cutting out cheeks, trimming and skinning the sterilized heads. The first four jobs are held by Negro men; a white man and a Negro cut out the cheeks, and the remaining jobs are performed by white

---

[1] For a detailed and authoritative statement of all occupations in the industry, see *Descriptions of Occupations, Slaughtering and Meat-Packing*, prepared for the United States Employment Service by the United States Bureau of Labor Statistics, 1918, and United States Department of Labor Bulletin No. 472, pp. 131-161.

[2] See pp. 117-118 for examples of division of labor.

men. Negro men in this same group cut out eyelids, split heads, grind and chop off the nostril, and grind out the teeth, the wage payments for these operations respectively being 45½ cents, 42½ cents, and piece-rates for the last two—40¼ cents a hundred pieces. Two white men receive 42½ cents an hour for pulling snouts and cutting eardrums. Women in a very limited number work at the same tables with the men or at adjoining ones. A Negro woman splits heads at the rate of 36 cents an hour; another, performing a more skilled task by machine and knife, receives 42½ cents. Two others, who are trimmers, are paid at the rate of 36 cents; a young Negro woman who saves brains receives 30 cents an hour. One white girl is paid 45½ cents an hour for cutting eardrums, while four more receive 36 cents for saving fat and ears, for cutting off nozzles, trimming snouts, shaving lips, and trimming tongues. In the hog head department the workers stand on brick floors with their backs against the wall, while a line of hogs moves steadily on not six feet distant. The light is artificial. Both the material and the surroundings are excessively damp.

In the adjoining room, the heads are put upon the machines which grind off the nostril and jaw bones, and send the teeth flying in every direction; and it is here, too, that the tongues are trimmed and the brains saved. But the main work in this rather small room is that of pulling and washing small and middle guts, pulling ruffle fat, washing cauld fat and tankage, separating plucks which consist of the heart, lungs, gullet, and weasand. Running water is a necessity and it freely overflows in every direction; the workers stand on wooden planks and wear boots and galoshes (which they furnish at their own expense), to protect themselves. The brick floor is painted red, and it is impossible to distinguish how much of the dampness on the floor is water and how much blood. The windows in the old building are small and dirty and afford no ventilation or sunlight. The ceiling is low, and the temperature high with the excessive heat from the next room. Wages range from 45½ cents paid to the women for pulling and washing ruffle fat and trimming flux, to 30 cents for trimming kidneys, cleaning stomachs, and splitting weasand meat. The weas-

and, after being cut from the paunch, is stripped of the gullet rings which have remained attached.   A lean strip of
meat, which is used in sausage, must be removed from the
gullet before it is sent to lard.   The bloody strips of meat
about an inch in diameter are pulled over a spike firmly
lodged in the center of a board.   When the spike is full,
a knife is run along the edge to split the meat.

The beef casing room, which adjoins the hog killing room,
always has a high temperature, ranging from 110° to 115°
in summer, and is steamy.   Excessive noise makes conversation almost impossible.   Odors are strong and repulsive.
Water streams upon the floor, which is always wet, and
flows from the sinks and troughs to the drains.   A strong
hose is used at frequent intervals during the day to clean
the refuse from the cement and bricks.   Ceilings are low,
the artificial light bulbs unshaded and inadequate to il-
luminate the room.   The few windows provide a bit of
natural light only for a bench of workers seated beneath
them.   The majority of the workers in this room are Negro
men.   Beef rounds, middles, and bungs must be carefully
cleaned and graded to be used as sausage casings.   The
amount of work depends entirely upon the number of animals slaughtered, the intestines coming through a chute
from the killing floor.

From the casing sets, the bungs are pulled and cut.   The
rounds and middles are pulled from the set and separated
from it and the ruffle fat.   From the casings the contents
are removed by the strippers, after which the fat is taken
from the outside and the slime or mucous lining from the
inner surface.   The casings are next turned by forcing water
through them; they are inflated then with water or air for
inspection and grading.   The rounds and middles are measured by length and put into bunches which are allowed to
stand in salt for about twenty-four hours.   They are then
removed and placed in the chill room ready for the market.
Most of the duct runners receive 54½ cents an hour; the
bung cutters, 58½ cents; and the middle-gut strippers, 47
cents an hour.   Those who remove the fat from the middles
are paid at the rate of $3.50 a hundred pieces.   The turners
and operators of the sliming machines receive 45½ cents

an hour. These operations require experienced workers. The department employs quite a large number of general workers, who are shifted about from one kind of cleaning to another, from casings and weasands, bladders and chitterlings, and earn from 45 to 50 cents an hour. In addition, there are numbers of unskilled laborers, roustabouts, and truckers.

Women do not work on the casings which have not been cleaned and slimed. After the bungs are cleaned, they are put in cold water and the warts or knots are removed with surgeons' shears. The bung trimmers, who are Polish women, receive 39½ cents an hour. Negro women inspect and measure all casings; the nine women inspecting in this particular plant receive from 30 to 42½ cents an hour. The work, which is performed at troughs, consists in pulling the end of casings over the water faucet for flooding and inspecting. A small amount of skill is required for this task, since requirements and specifications for each casing are definite. The casings are measured and put in salt. Although the women stand on boards, and wear boots, rubbers, or galoshes, they suffer from the dampness; their hands are in water all day. In this same room there are several small sinks at which women clean portions of the viscera.

A worker's time is often divided between the trimming and packing and the beef casing departments. Paid by piece-rate, trimming and packing are considered quite desirable by the Polish women who constitute the majority on the regular force. The women trim pieces of meat and prepare them for the market. They are in reality trimmers of trimmings, separating the lean from the fat and removing the rinds from fresh pork trimmings, hams, shoulders, and bellies. As each handles a particular cut removing the fat or lean, she becomes very skilled. As the meat is chilled when it comes to this group and must be kept at a low temperature, the workers must dress warmly. In addition to their heavy dresses, they usually wear sweaters, shawls, or pieces of burlap, and overshoes or galoshes and stand on elevated wooden platforms about three or four feet in height. From a room chill and damp, workers are often transferred for half a day to a room hot and humid.

APPENDIX D

LIST OF TABLES AND CHARTS IN *THE NEGRO IN THE SLAUGHTERING AND MEAT-PACKING INDUSTRY IN CHICAGO,* BY ALMA HERBST

Unpublished Doctoral Dissertation, 1930, University of Chicago, University of Chicago Library.

TABLES

I. Wage-Earners, by Months, for the United States and Illinois, 1919-25—Slaughtering and Meat-Packing

II. Departmental Distribution of Women Employees, by Race and Nativity, in a Slaughtering and Meat-Packing Establishment

III. Hourly Rate of Wages of Women Employees in a Meat-Packing Establishment; Number and per cent Distribution and Cumulative Percentages

IV. 'Median' Hourly Rate of Wages of Men Employees in Twenty-Four Slaughtering and Meat-Packing Establishments; Number and per cent Distribution and Cumulative Percentages

V-A. Daily Hours of White and Negro Men Employees in Twenty-Four Slaughtering and Meat-Packing Establishments

V-B. Percentage of Men Employees of Each Race Working Specified Daily Hours

V-C. Percentage of White and Negro Men Employees Working Specified Daily Hours

VI. Hours per Week of Men Employees in Twenty-Four Slaughtering and Meat-Packing Establishments; Number and per cent Distribution and Cumulative Percentages

VII-A. Hours per Week of White and Negro Men Employees in Twenty-Four Slaughtering and Meat-Packing Establishments

VII-B. Percentage of Men Employees of Each Race Working Specified Weekly Hours

VII-C. Percentage of White and Negro Men Employees Working Specified Weekly Hours

VIII. 'Median' Weekly Earnings of Men Employees in Twenty-Four Slaughtering and Meat-Packing Establishments; Number and per cent Distribution and Cumulative Percentages

IX. 'Median' Hourly Rate of Wages of Women Employees in Eighteen Slaughtering and Meat-Pack-

CHARTS

INDEX

Alschuler, Judge Samuel S., arbitrator of labor disputes in meat-packing industry, 38–40, 43, 48, 53

Amalgamated Meat Cutters and Butcher Workmen of North America, 21–22, 28, 32, 33, 37, 38, 43, 44, 51, 57, 58, 59, 61, 65, 66

American-born, employment in meat-packing industry, 14, 16, 30, 110

American Federation of Labor, attitude toward Negroes, 31; support of Butcher Workmen, 44

American Unity Labor Union, 35

American Unity Packers Union, 35–36, 62–63

American Unity Welfare League, 62–63

Applications for employment compared with accessions, see Employment

Arbitration of labor disputes in meat-packing industry, 38–40

Armour, J. Ogden, forms combination of packers, 1886, 15

Austrians, employment in meat-packing industry, 30

Bedoux Wage System, 114, 116–118

Bohemians, employment in meat-packing industry, 16

Bratton, I. H., Negro labor organizer, 33, 47, 52

Brennan, Redmond S., attorney for unions at arbitration hearings, 40

Canadians, employment in meat-packing industry, 30

Chicago Advocate, labor paper, 36

Chicago Federation of Labor, forms Stock Yards Labor Council, 29; tries to steady members during race riots, 47, 48, 62

Chicago race riots, 43, 45–47, 50–51

Children, employment in meat-packing industry, see Employment

Cincinnati, superseded as center of meat-packing industry by Chicago, 13

Commissioner of Corporations Report on Beef Industry, 9

Condon, J. J., attorney for packers at arbitration hearings, 40

'Consent decree', limiting commodities sold by packers, 9

Covington, Mrs. Laura Myrtle, testifies on working conditions of Negro women, 40

Conveyer system, operation in meat-packing industry, 7

Croatians, employment in meat-packing industry, 16, 18

DePriest, Oscar, Negro labor leader, 57

Discharge of labor union members, 16, 34

District Council No. 9, 28, 43–44

Dixon, Rev. Charles, speaking against subsidized anti-union Negroes, 64

Donnelly, Michael, labor organizer, 21, 31

Employee representation in meat-packing industry, 28, 54, 57–59; favorable attitude of Negroes toward, 60–61

Employment, applications for, compared with accessions, 106–108; Negroes compared with whites, 106–108; guarantee of,

high among unskilled and 'floaters', 142–144

Labor mobility, 71, Chapter VII, supra; definition, 128; rates in one meat-packing establishment, 132–133

Labor replacement rate, 71; comparison between Negroes and whites, 130–133; definition, 128

'Labor turnover', comparison between whites and Negroes not conclusive, 146–147; definition, 128; usual figures not of value in present study, 71

Leaving employment, reasons for, see Employment

Length of service in meat- packing industry, see Employment

Lewis, Freddie, first Negro employed in meat-packing industry, 16

Libby, McNeill and Libby Co., employment conditions, 40

Lithuanians, employment in meat-packing industry, 19, 22, 23, 30, 77

Living habits, undesirable among Negro meat-packing employees, 72–73

'Local [union] 651', 32, 42, 56, 60, 63

Magyars, employment in meat-packing industry, 16, 18

Meat-packing industry, division of labor in, 6–8, 69, 73, extent of, in Chicago, 3, 5, 6, 13, 151–152, in Illinois, 153–154, in the United States, 155–156; growth of, 13, 151–156; mechanization in, xvii, 7; specialization in, 7; speeding-up in, xvii, 7–9, 20, 21, 73; standardization in, xvii, 7, 23

Methods of investigation used in study, viii, xxi, 81, 92, 97–99, 110, 129–130

Mexicans, latest group of unskilled workers in meat-packing industry, xxii

Meyer, Carl, attorney for packers at arbitration hearings, 40

Morris, Nelson & Co., lodging strike-breakers, 23; warehouse fired, 18–19

National Council of defense, 38

Negroes, efficiency of, in meat-packing industry, xix–xx, 98, 127, 146–147; employment of, in meat-packing industry, see Employment; number of, in Chicago, 45; in meat-packing industry, xxi, 30, 101–103; proportion of, in meat-packing industry, xxi–xxii, 28, 76, 86, 100–101, 103, 110, Chart VI; wages of, in meat-packing industry, see Wages

Pace-setters in meat-packing industry, xx, 8, 20

Packers and Stockyards Act, 9

Packing Trades Council (of labor organizations), 23

Palmer-Packer agreement, 9

Parker, Richard, Negro labor agent, 35

Physical examination of applicants for employment in a packing plant, see Employment

Poles, employment in meat-packing industry, xvii, 15, 16, 17, 19, 22, 30, 77, 110

Powderley, T. V. and Knights of Labor in Stockyards strike of 1886, 15

President's Meditation Commission, 37

Processes in slaughtering and meat-packing industry, 4–5, 7, 74–80, 110, 112, 117–118, 166–171; carried on by Negroes, 74–80, 110, 112, 119–120

Promotion opportunities in meat-packing industry, xviii, 69–71; limited for Negroes, xviii–xix, 70

Racial antagonism, xix, 17–20, 34, 44, 98

Racial competition, xix, xxiii, 13–14, 16, 19, 21, 35, 55, 62, 105–109

Racial coöperation, 22, 50, 98

Racial discrimination, 40, 69, 75–76, 77–78, 103–104, 109, 112, 119–120, 125–126

Reed, George W., Negro labor organizer, 33, 65

Refrigeration, development of, 9–10

American Labor: From Conspiracy to Collective Bargaining

AN ARNO PRESS/NEW YORK TIMES COLLECTION

SERIES I

Abbott, Edith.
Women in Industry. 1913.

Aveling, Edward B. and Eleanor M. Aveling.
Working Class Movement in America. 1891.

Beard, Mary.
The American Labor Movement. 1939.

Blankenhorn, Heber.
The Strike for Union. 1924.

Blum, Solomon.
Labor Economics. 1925.

Brandeis, Louis D. and Josephine Goldmark.
Women in Industry. 1907. New introduction by Leon Stein and
    Philip Taft.

Brooks, John Graham.
American Syndicalism. 1913.

Butler, Elizabeth Beardsley.
Women and the Trades. 1909.

Byington, Margaret Frances.
Homestead: The Household of A Mill Town. 1910.

Carroll, Mollie Ray.
Labor and Politics. 1923.

Coleman, McAlister.
Men and Coal. 1943.

Coleman, J. Walter.
The Molly Maguire Riots: Industrial Conflict in the Pennsylvania Coal Region. 1936.

Commons, John R.
Industrial Goodwill. 1919.

Commons, John R.
Industrial Government. 1921.

Dacus, Joseph A.
Annals of the Great Strikes. 1877.

Dealtry, William.
The Laborer: A Remedy for his Wrongs. 1869.

Douglas, Paul H., Curtis N. Hitchcock and Willard E. Atkins, editors.
The Worker in Modern Economic Society. 1923.

Eastman, Crystal.
Work Accidents and the Law. 1910.

Ely, Richard T.
The Labor Movement in America. 1890. New Introduction by Leon Stein and Philip Taft.

Feldman, Herman.
Problems in Labor Relations. 1937.

Fitch, John Andrew.
The Steel Worker. 1910.

Furniss, Edgar S. and Laurence Guild.
Labor Problems. 1925.

Gladden, Washington.
Working People and Their Employers. 1885.

Gompers, Samuel.
Labor and the Common Welfare. 1919.

Hardman, J. B. S., editor.
American Labor Dynamics. 1928.

Higgins, George G.
Voluntarism in Organized Labor, 1930-40. 1944.

Hiller, Ernest T.
The Strike. 1928.

Hollander, Jacob S. and George E. Barnett.
Studies in American Trade Unionism. 1906. New Introduction by
Leon Stein and Philip Taft.

Jelley, Symmes M.
The Voice of Labor. 1888.

Jones, Mary.
Autobiography of Mother Jones. 1925.

Kelley, Florence.
Some Ethical Gains Through Legislation. 1905.

LaFollette, Robert M., editor.
The Making of America: Labor. 1906.

Lane, Winthrop D.
Civil War in West Virginia. 1921.

Lauck, W. Jett and Edgar Sydenstricker.
Conditions of Labor in American Industries. 1917.

Leiserson, William M.
Adjusting Immigrant and Industry. 1924.

Lescohier, Don D.
Knights of St. Crispin. 1910.

Levinson, Edward.
I Break Strikes. The Technique of Pearl L. Bergoff. 1935.

Lloyd, Henry Demarest.
Men, The Workers. Compiled by Anne Whithington and
Caroline Stallbohen. 1909. New Introduction by Leon Stein
and Philip Taft.

Lorwin, Louis (Louis Levine).
The Women's Garment Workers. 1924.

Markham, Edwin, Ben B. Lindsay and George Creel.
Children in Bondage. 1914.

Marot, Helen.
American Labor Unions. 1914.

Mason, Alpheus T.
Organized Labor and the Law. 1925.

Newcomb, Simon.
A Plain Man's Talk on the Labor Question. 1886. New Introduction
  by Leon Stein and Philip Taft.

Price, George Moses.
The Modern Factory: Safety, Sanitation and Welfare. 1914.

Randall, John Herman Jr.
Problem of Group Responsibility to Society. 1922.

Rubinow, I. M.
Social Insurance. 1913.

Saposs, David, editor.
Readings in Trade Unionism. 1926.

Slichter, Sumner H.
Union Policies and Industrial Management. 1941.

Socialist Publishing Society.
The Accused and the Accusers. 1887.

Stein, Leon and Philip Taft, editors.
The Pullman Strike. 1894-1913. New Introduction by the editors.

Stein, Leon and Philip Taft, editors.
Religion, Reform, and Revolution: Labor Panaceas in the Nineteenth
  Century. 1969. New Introduction by the editors.

Stein, Leon and Philip Taft, editors.
Wages, Hours, and Strikes: Labor Panaceas in the Twentieth Century.
  1969. New introduction by the editors.

Swinton, John.
A Momentous Question: The Respective Attitudes of Labor and Capital. 1895. New Introduction by Leon Stein and Philip Taft.

Tannenbaum, Frank.
The Labor Movement. 1921.

Tead, Ordway.
Instincts in Industry. 1918.

Vorse, Mary Heaton.
Labor's New Millions. 1938.

Witte, Edwin Emil.
The Government in Labor Disputes. 1932.

Wright, Carroll D.
The Working Girls of Boston. 1889.

Wyckoff, Veitrees J.
Wage Policies of Labor Organizations in a Period of Industrial Depression. 1926.

Yellen, Samuel.
American Labor Struggles. 1936.

SERIES II

Allen, Henry J.
The Party of the Third Part: The Story of the Kansas Industrial Relations Court. 1921. *Including* **The Kansas Court of Industrial Relations Law** (1920) by Samuel Gompers.

Baker, Ray Stannard.
The New Industrial Unrest. 1920.

Barnett, George E. & David A. McCabe.
Mediation, Investigation and Arbitration in Industrial Disputes. 1916.

Barns, William E., editor.
The Labor Problem. 1886.

Bing, Alexander M.
War-Time Strikes and Their Adjustment. 1921.

Brooks, Robert R. R.
When Labor Organizes. 1937.

Calkins, Clinch.
Spy Overhead: The Story of Industrial Espionage. 1937.

Cooke, Morris Llewellyn & Philip Murray.
Organized Labor and Production. 1940.

Creamer, Daniel & Charles W. Coulter.
Labor and the Shut-Down of the Amoskeag Textile Mills. 1939.

Glocker, Theodore W.
The Government of American Trade Unions. 1913.

Gompers, Samuel.
Labor and the Employer. 1920.

Grant, Luke.
The National Erectors' Association and the International Association of Bridge and Structural Ironworkers. 1915.

Haber, William.
Industrial Relations in the Building Industry. 1930.

Henry, Alice.
Women and the Labor Movement. 1923.

Herbst, Alma.
The Negro in the Slaughtering and Meat-Packing Industry in Chicago. 1932.

[Hicks, Obediah.]
Life of Richard F. Trevellick. 1896.

Hillquit, Morris, Samuel Gompers & Max J. Hayes.
The Double Edge of Labor's Sword: Discussion and Testimony on Socialism and Trade-Unionism Before the Commission on Industrial Relations. 1914. New Introduction by Leon Stein and Philip Taft.

Jensen, Vernon H.
Lumber and Labor. 1945.

Kampelman, Max M.
The Communist Party vs. the C.I.O. 1957.

Kingsbury, Susan M., editor.
Labor Laws and Their Enforcement. By Charles E. Persons, Mabel Parton, Mabelle Moses & Three "Fellows." 1911.

McCabe, David A.
The Standard Rate in American Trade Unions. 1912.

Mangold, George Benjamin.
Labor Argument in the American Protective Tariff Discussion. 1908.

Millis, Harry A., editor.
How Collective Bargaining Works. 1942.

Montgomery, Royal E.
Industrial Relations in the Chicago Building Trades. 1927.

Oneal, James.
The Workers in American History. 3rd edition, 1912.

Palmer, Gladys L.
Union Tactics and Economic Change: A Case Study of Three Philadelphia Textile Unions. 1932.

Penny, Virginia.
How Women Can Make Money: Married or Single, In all Branches of the Arts and Sciences, Professions, Trades, Agricultural and Mechanical Pursuits. 1870. New Introduction by Leon Stein and Philip Taft.

Penny, Virginia.
Think and Act: A Series of Articles Pertaining to Men and Women, Work and Wages. 1869.

Pickering, John.
The Working Man's Political Economy. 1847.

Ryan, John A.
A Living Wage. 1906.

Savage, Marion Dutton.
Industrial Unionism in America. 1922.

Simkhovitch, Mary Kingsbury.
The City Worker's World in America. 1917.

Spero, Sterling Denhard.
The Labor Movement in a Government Industry: A Study of Employee Organization in the Postal Service. 1927.

Stein, Leon and Philip Taft, editors.
Labor Politics: Collected Pamphlets. 2 vols. 1836-1932. New Introduction by the editors.

Stein, Leon and Philip Taft, editors.
The Management of Workers: Selected Arguments. 1917-1956. New Introduction by the editors.

Stein, Leon and Philip Taft, editors.
Massacre at Ludlow: Four Reports. 1914-1915. New Introduction by the editors.

Stein, Leon and Philip Taft, editors.
Workers Speak: Self-Portraits. 1902-1906. New Introduction by the editors.

Stolberg, Benjamin.
The Story of the CIO. 1938.

Taylor, Paul S.
The Sailors' Union of the Pacific. 1923.

U.S. Commission on Industrial Relations.
Efficiency Systems and Labor. 1916. New Introduction by Leon Stein and Philip Taft.

Walker, Charles Rumford.
American City: A Rank-and-File History. 1937.

Walling, William English.
American Labor and American Democracy. 1926.

Williams, Whiting.
What's on the Worker's Mind: By One Who Put on Overalls to Find Out. 1920.

Wolman, Leo.
The Boycott in American Trade Unions. 1916.

Ziskind, David.
One Thousand Strikes of Government Employees. 1940.

H/52
1911

Soc
E
185.8
H52
1971

DATE DUE

JUN 1 2 1978	
JUN 2 9 1981	SEP 1 5 1995
MAPR 1 9 1991	
MAR 1 4 1995	